Martyn Payne joined the *Barn*  worked with CMS as Nationa several years. Martyn has wide and churches to explore wa children.

Before his time with CMS, Martyn worked for 18 years as a teacher in East London, both leading a modern languages department and also being involved in the planning, writing and delivery of RE lessons. He has experience in producing materials for schools and has produced a large bank of flexible outlines, which have been widely used in the classroom.

Martyn has travelled in Europe, the Middle East and Africa, where he has also been involved in training children's workers and teachers. Martyn is an experienced workshop leader, Godly Play teacher and speaker and has collaborated with children's advisers and education officers in major school, church and family events across the UK. Based in London, he is available to lead RE days in schools, INSET training, church-based training sessions and workshops and help run special events throughout the UK. Martyn is author of *A-cross the World* (*Barnabas*, 2004).

Text copyright © Martyn Payne 2007
The author asserts the moral right
to be identified as the author of this work

**Published by**
**The Bible Reading Fellowship**
15 The Chambers, Vineyard
Abingdon OX14 3FE
Website: www.brf.org.uk

ISBN 978 1 84101 464 7
First published 2007
10 9 8 7 6 5 4 3 2 1 0
All rights reserved

**Acknowledgments**
Unless otherwise stated, scripture quotations are taken from the Contemporary English
Version of the Bible published by HarperCollins Publishers, copyright © 1991, 1992, 1995
American Bible Society.

Scripture quotations taken from the Holy Bible, New International Version, copyright ©
1973, 1978, 1984 by International Bible Society, are used by permission of Hodder &
Stoughton Limited. All rights reserved. 'NIV' is a registered trademark of International Bible
Society. UK trademark number 1448790.

Scriptures quoted from the Good News Bible published by The Bible Societies/HarperCollins
Publishers Ltd, UK © American Bible Society 1966, 1971, 1976, 1992, used with permission.

**Performance and copyright**
The right to perform *Footsteps to the Feast* drama material is included in the purchase price, so
long as the performance is in an amateur context, for instance in church services, schools or
holiday club venues. Where any charge is made to audiences, written permission must be
obtained from the author, who can be contacted through the publishers. A fee or royalties
may be payable for the right to perform the script in that context.

A catalogue record for this book is available from the British Library

Printed in Singapore by Craft Print International Ltd

# Footsteps
## to the Feast

12 two-hour children's programmes
for Christian festivals and special times of the year

Martyn Payne

*This book is dedicated to all those churches and fellowships around the country who have kindly invited me to come and lead events with children as part of their mission in their local area. I have learned so much from working with others and, of course, most from the children themselves.*

## Acknowledgment

*I would like to include a note of thanks to all the members of the Barnabas ministry team of BRF with whom I have worked for these last four years. Their encouragement and advice have been so important and, indeed, you will notice in some of the outlines that it is their inspiration and even some of their ideas that have helped bring this book to completion.*

## Photocopying permission

# Contents

Foreword ................................................................................................7

Introduction ..........................................................................................8

How to use this book ........................................................................9

Footsteps to the feast programme outline ..............................15

1   On your marks! ............................................................................16
    A children's or all-age event to celebrate Advent

2   Star time! ........................................................................................35
    A special event to celebrate the feast of Epiphany

3   Grandparents' day! ......................................................................51
    A special event to celebrate the feast of Candlemas

4   Fast forward! .................................................................................64
    A special event for the feast of Lent

5   The feast of feasts! ......................................................................80
    A special event for Holy Week

6   Can do day! ....................................................................................95
    A special event for the feast of Pentecost

7   3-2-1 Go! .......................................................................................110
    A special event for the feast of Trinity

8   Bible pioneers! ...........................................................................126
    A special event to celebrate the early Church,
    with a focus on St Barnabas

9. Thanks a million!................................................................................141
A special event to celebrate harvest festival

10. Light refreshment! ..........................................................................160
A special event for Hallowe'en and the feast of All Saints

11. God's messengers!...........................................................................178
A special event for the feast of St Michael and All Angels

12. Read all about it!.............................................................................194
A special event to celebrate Bible Sunday

Templates
Star lampshade.................................................................................226
Dove mobile ....................................................................................227
Flame template ................................................................................228
Bible labyrinth .................................................................................229

Bible index.......................................................................................230

Bibliography ....................................................................................232

# Foreword

The thing about Christian festivals is that they keep coming round each year. This rhythm is important because it helps us recall and celebrate the story of God's love, but it can sometimes stretch children's leaders who are trying to think of fresh, imaginative approaches time after time. Enter Martyn Payne, who has gathered together ideas he has used in local churches over the last twelve years.

*Footsteps to the Feast* not only offers creative approaches to Christian festivals throughout the year, but also gives opportunities to mark the 'getting ready' times of Advent, Lent and Holy Week, which sometimes get lost along the way. Each of the celebrations is designed to help children (and adults!) have fun while walking deeper into the Christian story. Drama, activity and craft are balanced with story, reflection, prayer and worship so that different pathways can be trodden depending on your local needs and resources.

Although designed as stand-alone programmes, the ideas in each session offer plenty of material which could be woven into the wider church's life and worship so that children and adults can walk (and run and explore and jump) along the path of faith together.

In James 4:8 we read, 'Come near to God, and he will come near to you.' *Footsteps to the Feast* is a welcome way to help both children and adults come near to God through the festival framework of the Christian year.

*Mary Hawes, National Children's Adviser for the Church of England*

# Introduction

Give a children's leader one good idea and it will soon multiply into two or three or four! This has been my experience during the last twelve years as a trainer with those who work with children in the church. They are a creative bunch, who are constantly on the lookout for new ways to pass on the stories of the Bible to those in their care, and new ways to take our story of faith out to other children in the community. Indeed, children's leaders have always been at the forefront when it comes to being mission-minded, ever exploring innovative ways to proclaim the gospel afresh to a new generation—a fact that the church has not always recognized.

It is with this understanding that I have gathered together the ideas in this book, confident that each chapter will spark off further inspiration and creativity in the minds of those who use it. During my years as National Children's Work Coordinator for the Church Mission Society and now as part of the *Barnabas* ministry team of BRF, I've had the privilege of working with children's leaders up and down the country, as together we have run special events for children and their carers that help to tell our gospel story. Again and again, when I have come along with an outline, I have seen my original ideas grow as the creative minds of the teams with whom I have worked have planned and developed the event.

The outlines for the events in *Footsteps to the Feast* are the product of just this sort of collaboration. Each of these festival specials started life as part of an event that was planned together by a local team and myself. I expect that some readers will recognize elements that first saw the light of day in a church or hall near to them.

Good ideas need to be shared, and so this book was born. I hope it will be of use to many churches around the country looking for new ways to engage the children in their area with the Christian faith. Some churches still have the ability to put on the grand enterprise of a week-long holiday club once a year, but for many this is no longer possible. However, the idea of special half-day events is much more within their reach. In my experience, this approach has opened up new possibilities for churches, providing contacts with children on a more evenly spaced programme across the year. It is also an approach that works well with the fact that many children, even those who are part of our church family, cannot regularly come to a weekly event. These occasional festival specials are another way for those children to 'footstep' their way into the faith, as well as being attractive celebrations that can draw others from outside the church.

*Footsteps to the Feast* is offered as material for just this sort of approach to children's work. In some cases, it may supplement the regular week-by-week diet while also enabling churches to reach a wider audience from time to time; for others it will provide a new way to pass on our faith by making use of the festival framework that already exists in the normal cycle of the Christian year.

I have enjoyed planning and leading these *Footsteps* specials and, as ever, working with children and their leaders, I have received far more than I have given. May this be your experience, too, as you use these outlines to help tell the good news of Jesus to the next generation.

## How to use this book

The twelve outlines for the special children's events in *Footsteps to the Feast* focus on Christian festivals and special days throughout the year. Each session is designed to last up to two hours and is ideal for a half-day event, perhaps at the weekend, in the school holidays or possibly an early-evening after-school session. The outlines are also evenly spaced throughout the year and so offer a range of possible slots, which you might choose from to tell the

Christian story on a regular basis. Some churches use a day in the half-term weeks as a convenient time to offer this sort of annual programme, thus providing up to three special days a year. Each church, however, needs to work out its own pattern and, of course, it will depend on the resources it has and the availability of leaders.

Each session outline contains a wealth of ideas to deliver a balanced programme, including:

- Background information to the feast itself.
- Warm-up activities.
- A festival chant.
- A selection of games.
- Ideas for storytelling, drama, music and craft activities.
- A format for reflection and worship together.

In addition, for each of the chapters, there are some further storytelling ideas on the *Barnabas* website , using a more reflective approach to handling scripture in the style known as *Godly Play*. (Visit www.barnabasinchurches.org.uk.)

Of course, you will need to gather a team to deliver these special events and, with them, plan carefully who will be responsible for each part of the programme. The team should include at least:

- An overall coordinator who will keep an eye on all aspects on the day as well as organizing the planning beforehand.
- One or two upfront leaders, who will take the opening warm-up session, and be responsible for the storytelling and possibly also the worship at the end.
- Leaders for the craft, music and drama workshops.
- Someone to coordinate the reflection and worship at the end, if this is not already being done by one of the upfront leaders.

In addition, there may need to be other leaders for registration, for the teams and as helpers with the workshops, all depending on the number of children involved at the event.

Each session outline includes a selection of ideas, so the first task of the team is to choose carefully from these ideas and plan the parts of the programme with which they want to work. In addition, they should take some time to read the Bible background together so that they are familiar with its content and fully aware of its potential for sharing and nurturing faith with children. Each chapter also contains suggestions for materials needed to deliver that session— items that may need to be bought or made for the day. The overall team coordinator should check that everything is in place.

The most important preparation for these events is prayer. It is vital to remember that these sessions are not designed just to entertain and occupy children but rather, through God's grace, to become a means of growing faith in the lives of those with whom we work. To this end, make sure that you keep your church fully informed of your plans so that they can support you, surrounding all your preparation, as well as the day itself, with their prayers.

The heart of each *Footsteps* session is the Bible story for that festival or feast day and the worship related to it. It is important that these two parts are given a priority and done well. The activities, games and other fun elements of the session are special, but what makes this day different from any other 'secular' children's event is that God's word is being shared and that there is an opportunity to come close to God in worship. All the other parts of the programme could be shortened in some way, but please don't cut down the Bible story and the worship.

Finally, templates are provided for some of the activities. They can be found on pages 226–229 of this book or can be downloaded from www.barnabasinchurches.org.uk. Pages 232–234 give a list of books with further ideas for crafts, music and drama. These books can be obtained through the *Barnabas* website, which has an 'Ideas' section that can supplement what is already in this book.

It is such a privilege to work with children and I hope you will be enriched and blessed by using outlines from this book. I never cease to be amazed at the very special promise that Jesus gives us all, namely that in receiving a child we receive more of him, and that in receiving Jesus, we receive the Father who sent him. The church has often underestimated or even ignored this fact. Giving to and receiving from a child is the way to grow in faith. May this be your experience, too!

## Contacting the publisher

BRF is a Christian charity committed to resourcing the spiritual journey of adults and children alike. BRF publishes Bible reading notes and books for adults and, under its children's imprint *Barnabas*, a wide range of books to resource the teaching of RE at Key Stages 1 and 2, as well as materials for children's leaders in churches. BRF can be contacted at:

15 The Chambers
Vineyard
Abingdon OX14 3FE
Tel: 01865 319700
Fax: 01865 319701
E-mail: enquiries@brf.org.uk
Website: www.brf.org.uk

## Safety guidelines for events involving children

The following is a simple checklist for teams who are planning special events with children. Make sure you work through this list with all members of your team before the event.

1. Ask to see the local church or Diocesan Child Protection Policy and work within its guidelines. A Criminal Record Bureau (CRB) form will need to be signed and references provided for all those taking any leadership role on the day. It is also strongly recommended that leaders have experienced

some training for working with children. Sessions from *Core Skills for Children's Work*, published by *Barnabas*, are ideal for this purpose.

2.  Be aware of the recommended ratio of adults to children. A minimum of eight children to one adult is advisable for children aged eight and over. There should be more adults if the children are younger or if an activity takes place away from the usual premises.

3.  Children should always be accompanied if, for some reason, they have to leave the group. However, a male leader should not take girls to the toilet.

4.  Do not take responsibility for children without written permission from parents or guardians. Pre-registration forms are recommended, which include contact and phone numbers and any medical information.

5.  Exits and entrances to the venue should be stewarded and all those who are leaders should be identified in some way so that the children know who is 'safe'.

6.  A First Aid qualification should be held by at least one adult leader present for every 50 children at the event. Accidents should be recorded and reported to the person in overall charge.

7.  Simple general safety rules should be clearly set out, especially concerning movement about the building, refreshments, going to the toilet and being quiet for important announcements.

8.  Have a designated overall leader for the event, who takes final responsibility for safety, security and any pastoral issues that may arise.

9.  Insurance for the event should be checked. This may be covered either by the local church (through EIG Parishguard, for example) or by an external organization leading the event. Involvement of the Local Authority is necessary only if the event involves children aged eight or under for more than two hours a day on six or more days in the year.

10. Junior leaders (aged under 18) should not be left in charge of any activity or workshop involving children.

# Outline for a two-hour programme

| | |
|---|---|
| 00.00–00.15 | **First steps**<br>Welcome, opening warm-up activity, general introduction to the feast and learning the special chant. |
| 00.15–00.25 | **First footing**<br>Brief introduction to the story. |
| 00.25–00.40 | **Footbridge**<br>Theme game as a whole group together. |
| 00.40–01.00 | **Best foot forward**<br>Walking through the story using visual aids. |
| 01.00–01.10 | **Footrest**<br>Refreshment break (drink and biscuits). |
| 01.10–01.40 | **Footprints**<br>Drama, music and craft activities: each group of children spends approximately 10 minutes with each activity, rotating to the next activity after that time. |
| 01.40–01.45 | **Foothold**<br>Time of reflection and prayer. |
| 01.45–01.50 | **Footsteps to the feast**<br>A final game. |
| 01.50–02.00 | **Stepping out**<br>End with a feast together, which grandparents and parents can join. After this, the children can collect their craft work and go home. |

# On your marks!

## A children's or all-age event to celebrate Advent

It's hard for all of us to have to wait for something special to happen, and this is especially true for children. However, the Christian Church has a long tradition of setting aside 'times of waiting' as a preparation for the great feasts of faith. Advent is one of those times.

Christmas, with its central story of God becoming human, is too important a festival for us just to stumble into it without being ready. The four weeks of Advent, which trace the story of how God planned long ago the great mystery of the incarnation, aim to help us be properly prepared for the great celebration ahead. The hopes of the patriarchs, the promises of our powerful God and the words of the prophets are recalled as we build up to the birth in the Bethlehem stable.

In contrast, the secular and commercial world's build-up to the Christian holiday break increasingly dominates the lives of our children, who are influenced by the hope of expensive presents, the promise of special foods and the glitter of the adverts luring them on to the New Year sales. For most children today, the Advent calendar is no more than a 24-compartment chocolate box that has nothing to do with the Bible story.

The following outline for an Advent party event aims to put the scriptural story of this 'getting ready' time back on centre-stage. It can be used at any suitable time in the weeks of December in order to help children arrive at the festival prepared for and excited by the true meaning of Christmas. Using this outline, you will also be able to link the drama element into an opportunity to develop and rehearse a presentation for a special nativity service to take place on the Sunday before Christmas itself. It isn't always easy to do this during normal Sunday group meeting time, especially if attendance is variable. Building it in as part of this event, leading to a special service, also carries the hope of drawing in new families to your Christmas celebrations.

## Bible footsteps

The story can be found in Isaiah 6:1—9:7 and Luke 1:5—2:19.

# First steps

As children arrive and are registered, they should be put into four groups, each with a team base and team leaders. The team names and team bases should be linked to different parts of the Bible that point us forward to the coming of Jesus. Here are some suggested names:

- ❂ **Pioneers:** These are the patriarchs, whose stories and promises foreshadow the coming of Jesus.
- ❂ **Rulers:** These are the kings, whose lives point us to the coming king.
- ❂ **Messengers:** These are the prophets, whose words describe what Jesus' coming will be like.
- ❂ **Heralds:** These are events and people, such as the birth of John the Baptist and the words at the annunciation, that immediately precede the birth of the baby at Christmas.

Each team base should include a large signpost along with other visuals and Bible verses to highlight the various pieces of the Advent jigsaw that come together at Christmas. Examples are given overleaf.

17

## Pioneers

**Signpost:** A special leader.
**Visuals:** Names of the patriarchs (Abraham, Isaac, Jacob and Moses).
**Bible promises:** Everyone on earth will be blessed because of you (Genesis 12:3b); He will choose one of your own people to be a prophet (Deuteronomy 18:15a).

## Rulers

**Signpost:** A special king.
**Visuals:** Names of Bible kings (David, Solomon and Ahaz).
**Bible promises:** I will keep my promise to David that someone from your family will always be king of Israel (1 Kings 9:5); I have helped a mighty hero. I chose him from my people and made him famous (Psalm 89:19).

## Messengers

**Signpost:** A special person.
**Visuals:** Names of some of the prophets, such as Isaiah, Jeremiah and Micah.
**Bible promises:** A child has been born for us. We have been given a son who will be our ruler (Isaiah 9:6); Some day I will appoint an honest king from the family of David, a king who will be wise and rule with justice (Jeremiah 23:5); Bethlehem Ephrath, you are one of the smallest towns in the nation of Judah. But the Lord will choose one of your people to rule the nation—someone whose family goes back to ancient times (Micah 5:2).

## Heralds

**Signpost:** A miracle child.
**Visuals:** Names of those whom God's angel visited just before Jesus came into the world (Zechariah, Mary and Joseph).

**Bible promises:** Our God has given us a mighty Saviour from the family of David his servant (Luke 1:69); He helps his servant Israel and is always merciful to his people. The Lord made this promise to our ancestors, to Abraham and his family for ever! (Luke 1:54–55).

Once all the children have arrived, gather them together for some warm-up exercises on the theme of 'getting ready'. For example, include some rapid and repeated mime for the following situations:

⚙ Getting ready to go on holiday
⚙ Getting ready to go to a party
⚙ Getting ready to take an important penalty kick
⚙ Getting ready for an Olympic final
⚙ Getting ready for a grand meal

Make this fun and fast moving!

You might also practise a few 'on your marks, get set, go' routines in various poses: for example, runners in a race, swimmers at the Olympic pool, cyclists, cricketers and so on.

Give a short introduction to the theme.

Part of the fun of special events is, of course, getting ready, but some things take longer to get ready for than others. God spent a very long time indeed getting ready for the miracle of Christmas— not just the four weeks before the day, but all the years since the very beginning of time. This unique moment in the Christian story didn't just happen. God gave hints and signposts to what he was about to do.

Today we are going to explore this time of getting ready, which we call Advent, as we move towards Christmas itself. Advent seems to be suggesting that the very best things come not just to those who wait, but also to those who are ready.

Amazingly, however, even though God had given so many clues

as to what was about to come, most people were not ready when it did happen; they were taken by surprise. Very few had been able to work out what God was really going to do at Christmas to rescue the world he loves.

## Footsteps chant

Here is a special Advent chant that you could use during the day as you move from one activity to another, or if you want to call the whole group together. Initiate a simple clapping rhythm and then have the children echo each line of the poem after you, repeating this several times, varying pace and volume.

*We're on a special journey*
*Of stories from the Book.*
*To see how God surprised us all,*
*Let's take a closer look.*

# First footing

Advent is a time to recall, one by one, the stages in the Bible story that lead up to the moment when God sent Jesus into the world. As the apostle Paul writes, 'when the time was right, God sent his Son' (Galatians 4:4). It seemed like a very long wait, but God in his grace took the trouble to prepare the world for what was about to happen. In the same way as we, on a much smaller scale, have to prepare and plan for Christmas (the meals, the presents, decorating the tree and so on), God prepared for Christmas Day.

There are clues to God's great rescue plan right throughout the Old Testament and, in some ways, Advent is like a treasure hunt as we search for and put together all these clues. As a way into today's story, you will need to collect pictures of the items below. They can be printed off from the Internet or computer clipart. Each one is a visual clue about how God will send Jesus.

You will need to make as many sets of these images as there are teams. Then, the pictures should be hidden around your meeting area for the Advent treasure hunt. Have a large sheet of paper, scissors and glue for each group so that they can make their pictures into a collage once they have collected all twelve images.

☺ **A star-filled sky:** representing God's promise of a worldwide family of faith one day (Genesis 22:17).
☺ **A roaring lion:** representing God's promise to the tribe of Judah about a ruler who would come (Genesis 49:9–10).
☺ **A royal crown:** representing God's promise of a future king like David, but one who would last for ever (Psalm 89:27–29).
☺ **A tiny baby:** representing God's promise to Isaiah of a special child who would have amazing names (Isaiah 9:6).
☺ **The branch of a tree:** representing God's promise of a special rescuer who would bring new growth and life for God's people (Jeremiah 23:5–6).
☺ **A village:** representing God's promise that this would all happen in a small place called Bethlehem (Micah 5:2–3).
☺ **A sheep:** representing God's promise that he would send an innocent victim to tackle death on our behalf (Genesis 22:13–14).
☺ **A group of camels:** representing God's promise that there would be visitors arriving with gifts from far-off countries (Isaiah 60:5b).
☺ **A man speaking to others:** representing the special prophet that God promised to Moses (Deuteronomy 18:18).
☺ **A picture of John the Baptist:** representing God's promise that he would send a messenger to prepare the way (Isaiah 40:3).
☺ **A little child:** representing God's promise that a child would usher in a new beginning for the world (Isaiah 11:6).
☺ **A shepherd:** representing God's promise that this new person would know how to care for us in a gentle way (Isaiah 40:11).

Once each team has collected all twelve clues, take some moments to run through the different images and see how they are clues to the coming of Jesus. Finally, work with the children on making the twelve images into a single picture by cutting and pasting as a collage on a large sheet of paper.

## Footbridge

Here are some games to play as a group on the theme of Advent.

**1.** How good are you at keeping still and waiting for something? Waiting even for a very short time can be quite a challenge. Tell the children that they must walk quietly in silence around the room, but once they think a certain period of time is up, they should sit down immediately on the ground. The leader tells them the times they need to estimate, varying between half a minute and one and a half minutes. The leader calls out when the actual time has passed. Who was closest to sitting down at the right moment?

**2.** Waiting—at least in Great Britain—is usually a case of standing in a queue. Challenge each team to form a queue, but according to certain criteria. For example:

❂ A queue in height order, the smallest at the front.
❂ A queue in age order, the oldest at the front.
❂ A queue according to the day on which the team members were born, with Sunday at the front.
❂ A queue in order of how many people are in their family at home, with the biggest number at the front.

You could try asking that some of these queues be formed in silence. It is interesting to see how a group reacts to this, and how they quickly learn to 'talk' with their hands.

**3.** Challenge your teams to get one person among them ready for a fancy dress party. To do this, each team member will have to fetch an item of clothing from the other end of the room. Collect together four or more equal piles of clothes, including things like hats, scarves, jackets, overtrousers, ties, huge shoes, embarrassing socks and so on—the more colourful and oversized, the better. When the game starts, one team member at a time runs up to the clothes pile and collects one item only to bring back and start dressing their 'lucky' teammate. Once that person has arrived with his or her item of clothing, the next person can go, and so on. You could introduce other elements to this game, such as an obstacle course to run through towards the clothes, only being allowed to run to certain rules or with a handicap, or blindfolding the person who is being dressed.

**4.** Another application of the 'getting ready' theme is a countdown. Challenge the group to form themselves into a unified team sculpture of various items, while the overall leader counts down from 5 to 1 (or maybe, for more complicated sculptures, 10 to 1). Teams could be challenged to make a sculpture in that time of:

❂ A space rocket
❂ Marathon runners at a start line
❂ A racing car
❂ Swimmers under starter's orders
❂ A church building
❂ A table laid for a meal
❂ A tent in the desert

## Best foot forward

Some of the Old Testament passages most often quoted at Advent come from the book of Isaiah. Over 500 years before Jesus was born, national events affecting the life of the kingdom of Judah, as well as personal events in the prophet's own life, became not only significant for the people of the time but also pointers to the mystery of the incarnation to come. These events and prophecies are recorded in Isaiah 6:1 to 9:7.

It is interesting that the outworkings of God's purposes at this point in history are all associated with the birth of children. Isaiah's own son's name is linked to the prophecy of hope and faith that God spoke to him on the day when he was overwhelmed by God's presence in the temple (see 6:1–11 and 7:3); a second child is named Emmanuel (which means 'God with us') along with the added warning that, before this child is about seven years of age (see 7:13–17), the nation will be in serious trouble; a third son has the longest name in the Bible, and this points forward to the awful day when the superpower of Assyria will overwhelm the kingdom of Judah (see 8:1–4); finally, a fourth child is spoken of, who has some incredible and mysterious names (see 9:6–7). Isaiah is now talking about something well beyond his own time, and Christians see this event as the birth of Christ, who brought light and joy into the world. Isaiah says that this fourth child will come from Galilee in the north, which is where Mary first heard the news that she was to be the mother of God.

These few chapters contain a whole heap of clues preparing us for Christmas.

Tell the following story of Isaiah to the children, inviting their participation with sound effects, reactions to the events and simple mime suggested by the words in bold.


Isaiah was a priest many hundreds of years before the first Christmas, but through the things that happened to him, God was preparing the world for what Christmas really means.

One day in the temple, Isaiah heard **angels singing**. He was **terrified** and felt that he didn't deserve to be there at all. But God wanted him to be a messenger. God warned him that he would be saying some things that **very few**

**would understand**. God promised Isaiah that, despite all that happened, there would be the **hope** of a new start one day. Because of God's message, Isaiah even gave his first son a name that meant something like 'hope one day'.

King Ahaz of Judah was **in a terrible panic**. The nearby countries of Syria and Israel wanted to force him to join them in a war against the superpower of the day, called Assyria. If he didn't do that, they threatened to get rid of him. Along with the whole country, the king was **paralysed with fear**. Isaiah knew what God wanted him to say. 'Trust in God' was Isaiah's message; 'if you don't, then the future's bleak.' Despite this message, King Ahaz **couldn't make up his mind**. But God sent a sign anyway, in the shape of a **baby** called Emmanuel, which means 'God with us'. It was God's way of saying that only by **trusting in God** being with them would there be any **hope** of a tomorrow. This is still true today, and Emmanuel was the name given by the angel to Jesus at Christmas.

Isaiah warned that before this child was about seven years old, Assyria would have beaten them all. Isaiah's second child was given the longest name ever! In English it means something like **'Quick, grab what you can; loot the lot'** (and you think a child named after an entire football team is sad!). It was Isaiah's dramatic way of warning everyone that things were going to be really bad. The enemy would get them all in the end. Indeed, within months of this birth, Syria and Israel were **swept away**, and not many years later Judah followed.

But Isaiah kept telling the people that if only they could **trust** in Emmanuel ('God with us'), things could be different. He went on to say that one day another child would be born. This child would be born in the north of the country. This child would bring **light into the darkness**. This child would bring joy. This child would change everything. This child would be given incredible names, such as Wonderful, Counsellor, Mighty God, Everlasting Father and Prince of Peace.

No one at the time understood what Isaiah was talking about. Maybe even Isaiah wasn't that sure what it all meant. But it was a clue: it was God's signpost pointing to Christmas. This was going to be God's great plan to send Jesus, whose name means 'rescuer'. This time it wasn't just Judah that could be rescued, but the whole world.

You might wish to consider ending this retelling by playing 'For unto us a child is born' from Handel's *Messiah*.

## Footrest

At this point in the programme, take a break for a drink and biscuits. Those who finish eating and drinking quickly could return to their bases and help decorate the signpost and work on other visuals there.

## Footprints

Now there is an opportunity for the group to experience up to three different activities, depending on the time available. The suggested three workshops are based around drama ('Footlights'), music ('Footnotes') and craft ('Fancy footwork').

In this part of the event, you could include the opportunity for one group, or all of them, to prepare and rehearse a presentation for a nativity play to be performed at the service nearest to Christmas. This would also be a good time to introduce and practise any new Christmas music that might go with the play. In the following outlines, there are ideas for resources for such a presentation.

## Footlights

Play some simple warm-up games with the group to get them ready for working on a short piece of drama for Advent and Christmas. Some suggestions are given below.

**1.** Advent is all about waiting. Begin by encouraging activities such as twiddling thumbs, yawning and stretching, looking anxiously around, and adopting puzzled and impatient looks. Then, on a sudden clap of the leader's hands, all should freeze into a position of shock and surprise, because the thing they been waiting for suddenly happens.

**2.** In small groups of three or four, ask the children to develop a mime in which they are waiting for something—for example, in a restaurant, at a bus stop, outside a sports ground or concert venue, or in a shop queue. After a minute or so of the mime, the group should stop the scene as a freeze frame (a still photo). Can the others guess where they are waiting?

**3.** With younger children, explore the build-up to a surprise. Mime with them the actions of slowly opening a mysterious door, gradually peeping out from under the bedclothes at night, cautiously opening a treasure chest or nervously pulling back the curtains. Then, at a given signal, everyone should react with huge surprise at what is seen. Ask the children for ideas about what it is they have seen.

**4.** Play a fruit salad type of game based around the animals of Advent. Give each child one animal name (sheep, donkey or camel), and encourage some practice at appropriate animal noises. Now call out one of those words: the children allocated that name have to cross the circle, while one or two volunteers in the middle try to grab a place in the circle for themselves while the others are moving—thus stranding someone else in the middle. If you want them all to move, call out the words 'Advent animals'.

Advent is the build-up to God's surprise for the world. God had been preparing for this event from the beginning of time. Our world needs rescuing from all that is bad. To do this, God did not send a mighty warrior or a superhero but a tiny baby. This was the great surprise. There had been clues about the coming of a new leader, a perfect king and a special rescuer throughout the Old Testament, but no one had really understood them. Now, in this workshop, it is time to focus on the surprise itself: the first Christmas.

Set the children walking around the room in different moods that they can practise for use in a drama of the nativity story. For example:

⊙ As bored people up on a hillside, on night duty with their sheep.
⊙ As nervous people down in the town under the watchful eyes of the Romans supervising the census.
⊙ As frightened people who have just seen thousands of angels.
⊙ As angry people who can't find anywhere to stay in the busy streets and inns of Bethlehem.
⊙ As puzzled people who have been disturbed by the noisy visit of the shepherds to the stable.
⊙ As searching people, looking up at a strange star in the sky.
⊙ As amazed people who discover God's great surprise.

Now divide the group up to work on some short improvised dramas under the overall title 'Taken by surprise'. You could tackle all the scenes in one workshop each time, or divide the scenes up among the workshop opportunities you have, so that different groups prepare different parts of the story. The different parts could then be drawn together later as your nativity presentation. Gather a few simple props for each scene as suggested below. Trust the children to create some dialogue and actions for each of these scenes.

- **The kitchen surprise**: Gabriel meets with Mary and, later, Mary talks with Joseph. You will need some kitchen items around a table and some indication of traditional Middle Eastern dress.
- **The hillside surprise**: The angels appear to the shepherds. You will need some indication of traditional Middle Eastern dress and some toy sheep.
- **The stable surprise**: Jesus is born among the animals at the back of the inn. You will need a box for the manger, some straw, animal masks and some indication of traditional Middle Eastern dress.

If you would prefer a scripted version of a nativity, *Barnabas* has a wide range of nativity drama ideas, some of which also include new songs for Christmas. See the bibliography on page 232 for a list of resources.

## Footnotes

There is no shortage of music for the Advent and Christmas season. This workshop will be an ideal place to rehearse traditional favourites as well as introducing some new songs. Songs could be sung just for this day's programme or, as in the drama workshop above, songs could be practised to go with the nativity play, ready for a presentation at a service in church. There are some splendid new songs in *Barnabas* publications (see the bibliography on page 232).

## Fancy footwork

Alongside the craft idea below, you may also wish to explore books in the *Barnabas* range that provide suggestions for things to make at this time of year. (See page 232 for details.)

### Advent signposts

**You will need** cardboard tubes from kitchen rolls, pieces of stiff card cut as long pointed signs, paints and/or colouring materials.

Cut small slits in the top of the cardboard tubes, into which the signpost arms will fit. Decorate the signposts and the signs themselves, adding words such as 'Advent signpost' or 'On your marks, get set!' for the main pole. On the signs, add some simple headline words that indicate the ways in which the Old Testament points forward to Jesus, such as 'A special leader', 'A special king', 'A special person' and 'A miracle child'.

## Foothold

Use the Footsteps chant (see page 20) to draw everyone together for a final time of reflection on the Advent theme. Each group should gather in a circle at their team base with their leaders. In the centre of each circle, you will need a simple Advent wreath with four candles around the edge and a large white candle in the centre. The four outside Advent candles are usually purple, but your church tradition may include a rose candle among the four. You will also need a candle snuffer and safety matches or a candle lighter.

Ask the groups to choose five people who will help a leader to light the candles, and another five who will snuff out the candles at the end. This will happen at the appropriate moments as indicated in the following simple liturgy, which can be read either by each leader for their own group or centrally by one leader for all. Point out that the names needed for each part of the liturgy are displayed in the team areas. Wait until everyone is quiet and settled before you begin.

**Leader:** Today we have been celebrating the season of Advent—the time of getting ready for the unexpected surprise of Christmas, which God planned long ago.

    God spoke to one family. That family grew into a tribe of people known as the Hebrews. To the great leaders of these people, God promised that one day an even greater leader would come.

*Light the first candle. Pause to enjoy the light before saying the words below together.*

**All:** Thank you for speaking to Abraham, Isaac, Jacob and Moses about Jesus, who is coming.

**Leader:** God spoke to one nation—the people of God. To the kings of this people, God promised that one day a special king would come.

*Light the second candle. Pause to enjoy the light before saying the following words together.*

**All:** Thank you for speaking to David, Solomon, Ahaz and others about Jesus, who is coming.

**Leader:** God spoke to the people of Judah and Israel, telling them to trust in God who was with them.

Through the prophets, God promised that one day a special person would come.

*Light the third candle. Pause to enjoy the light before saying the following words together.*

**All:**  Thank you for speaking through Isaiah, Jeremiah, Micah and others about Jesus, who is coming.

**Leader:**  God spoke to ordinary people among this special family, both in Jerusalem and Nazareth. To them, God promised that very soon he would send a miracle child.

*Light the fourth candle. Pause to enjoy the light before saying the following words together.*

**All:**  Thank you for speaking to Zechariah, Mary and Joseph about Jesus, who is coming.

**Leader:**  And then God sent his great surprise, born in Bethlehem in a cattle shed. Shepherds and angels worshipped together the gift of Jesus to the world.

*Light the central candle. Pause to enjoy the light before saying the following words together.*

**All:**  Jesus is coming. Jesus has come. And Jesus will come to us all.

*Now pass the snuffer around to those who have been chosen to 'change' the light. As they do this, say the following words.*

Reproduced with permission from *Footsteps to the Feast* published by BRF 2007 (978 1 84101 464 7).

**Leader:** As the smoke spreads, so the story of Advent and Christmas has been passed around the world. Jesus came to bring peace on earth and good news for everyone.

*Watch the smoke drifting from the five candles for a while and then begin a slower, more reflective version of the Footsteps chant to end the session. Do take care as the groups move away from where the candles are, back to the centre of the hall.*

## Footsteps to the feast

Gather the children in a large circle as a final act before the finish of the programme. Everyone should hold hands, including the leaders. When this large circle is ready, have everyone stand still, and explain that you are all going to act out the surprise of Christmas that no one expected. This is how it goes:

God, who is greater and bigger than we can ever imagine or understand, decided to wrap himself up very small so that he could come alongside us and love us. This circle is huge, but we are now going to make it small to show how Christmas is about the great surprise and miracle of God becoming a baby.

Ask the children to pull closer together and then slowly shuffle forward towards the centre, gradually contracting the circle (taking care, of course, not to push or hurry any younger and smaller children). Do this until you all become as tight a huddle of people as is possible, and safe. When you are in this position, say:

This is what God did. The most high became the most low. The Almighty became the all-tiny out of love for you and me. Because of this, God is able to help us to become the best we can be. This was God's surprising way of rescuing his world and remaking it again.

As you say these words, ask them all to expand the circle again very slowly and carefully to its full extent.

Finish the exercise by repeating the Footsteps chant, but changing the last line to 'It's here that we have looked.'

## Stepping out

Conclude the event with a feast, inviting parents and carers to join you for some seasonally appropriate food and drink. This might also be a good time to have a small Advent gift ready for each child to mark today's footsteps and to include an invitation to the coming nativity service. (See page 233 for *Barnabas* books about the Christmas story that would make ideal presents.)

# Star time!

## A special event to celebrate the feast of Epiphany

It is not unusual for some children's groups to celebrate the arrival of the New Year with a post-Christmas party in early January. If this is an annual custom in your church, why not make it into a special event to celebrate the feast of Epiphany, which begins on 6 January? This is the day when the Christian Church remembers the arrival of the wise men to visit the child Jesus in his home (no longer a stable) in Bethlehem. They had travelled from the east, so Epiphany, which means 'revelation', represents the moment when the light of Jesus was revealed to the world beyond Israel. The wise men (or magi) followed a star, hence the title for this special event: 'Star time!'

Stars also afford us further insights into the meaning of Epiphany within the Christian tradition. The stars flung into the sky at creation (Genesis 1:16)—far more than Abraham could count—represent the worldwide promised family of faith that would come one day (Genesis 15:5), the prophet Daniel writes that the witnesses or evangelists who turn many to righteousness are like stars that have proclaimed the gospel throughout the world (Daniel 12:3); finally, in the last book of the Bible, we see Jesus holding the stars of the churches, the new family of faith spread out throughout the world. These are the people who have seen the light of Christ rise in their hearts like the morning star (Revelation 1:16; 22:16).

The season of Epiphany picks up on this theme with two of the early Gospel stories, which are usually told at this time of year: the baptism of Christ, when his divinity was revealed to the world, and the story of the wedding at Cana, when the water-into-wine miracle also revealed his glory.

Stars are a useful theme for today's programme in other ways, too. We live in an age of showbiz stars and 'star quality'. The media world of the 21st century thrives on the cult of instant stardom, enticing us to look out for the next big star on the celebrity scene. Today's event aims to make clear that, for Christians, the only lasting star to whom Epiphany points is Jesus, who has come to reveal grace and truth to the world.

## Bible footsteps

The stories can be found in Genesis 12:1–9 and Matthew 2:1–12.

## First steps

Decorate the venue with stars of all shapes and sizes. If possible, attach some fluorescent stars to the ceiling and walls (these will be useful in the retelling of the story later, as they should glow when the lights are turned down). There are also star-shaped tealight candles, which could be arranged in safe places out of reach. Finally, set up one large star as a focus at the front.

As the children are registered, divide them into star groups, each with a leader at each star base, which they can decorate with yet more stars of their own. The teams could have names based on constellations or other star-related words such as starship, starchart, starlight, stargate, stardate, startrail and even, maybe, starbucks!

Another possible activity to occupy the group until everyone has arrived would be to hunt for particular 'stars' hidden around the room. Clues to these stars could be in the form of words or pictures, such as:

- A TV talent show (*Stars in their Eyes*)
- A science-fiction TV series (*Star Trek*)
- An epic set of space films (*Star Wars*)
- A star nursery rhyme (*Twinkle, twinkle, little star*)
- A posh hotel (*Five star*)

You could also put up pictures of various media stars, to be identified from their eyes only.

Once everyone has arrived, gather the children together and continue the star theme with some star-related warm-ups: for example, plenty of star jumps or opening and closing hands to make 'stars that twinkle'.

Play a game that involves children adopting particular shapes whenever certain star words are mentioned. Teach the words and the actions that go with them (see below). Play some music (perhaps from the *Star Wars* films) as they walk around the room. When the music stops, the children should freeze on the spot and then adopt the appropriate position. For example:

- Black hole (curl up into as tight a ball as possible)
- Supernova (come together in one great big group hug)
- White dwarf (walk around in a squatting position)
- Galaxy (link up in chains of five or six)
- Shooting stars (run at top speed on the spot)
- Stardust (lie still on the floor)

## Footsteps chant

Teach everyone a simple chant, which you can use throughout the event as you move people between activities or gather them together for the next stage of the programme. Start a rhythmical clapping and then ask everyone to repeat each line of the following poem after you. Repeat this several times, varying the speed and volume.

*We're on a starlit journey*
*Of stories from the Book.*
*To find the light which shines for all,*
*It's here we're going to look.*

## First footing

Introduce the group to the theme of the event: 'Star time!' Today's theme focuses on a moment in history when one very bright star was used as a sign that God had sent Jesus into our world as a baby. It was God's special spotlight on his gift of love to us all, a gift that he had promised right back at the beginning of creation. We find the story in Matthew 2:1–12.

Although many people must have seen this star when it first shone, it seems that only a group of star watchers from the east paid any real attention to it and were moved to investigate what it might mean. To them, it signified the arrival of a new king, so they brought extraordinary gifts that, like the star itself, would point to what sort of king the child would become.

Gold, frankincense and myrrh were the very best that these wise men could offer, and certainly suited someone who might be a rich ruler, an adored leader and someone who would bring health and wholeness to the world. Myrrh, however, the last of the gifts, although associated with healing, was also used to anoint the body of a person who had died.

Talking of gifts—and because this event comes so soon after Christmas—ask the children what made them choose the gifts they gave to their family and friends. Was it because they would like to get those presents themselves, or because they would suit the other person? As you talk about the gifts that the wise men brought, have some items wrapped to represent the gold, frankincense and myrrh, and show how these items pointed to who Jesus really was.

It is interesting to speculate whether the wise men realized how their special gifts would be interpreted. Did they know that this new child would bring spiritual wealth to the world? Did they understand what sort of humble leader he would turn out to be, and how he would be worshipped? Did they foresee what sort of healer he would become, and how different his death was going to be?

Like the star, Jesus was also destined to be a sign, shining with the light and love that would bring people close to God. Draw the group into the theme with some of these questions:

❂ I wonder why other people didn't also follow the star?
❂ I wonder why the wise men chose these particular gifts?
❂ I wonder what gifts you would have chosen to bring to a new baby king?
❂ I wonder what Mary and Joseph thought when these gifts were unwrapped?
❂ I wonder what they did with the gold, frankincense and myrrh?

## Footbridge

Here are some star games that you could use with your group.

**1.** In groups of four or five, ask the children to create their own particular star shapes according to the number of points of the star you ask for. They could do this by linking themselves up with their hands and creating points in the circle they are in, or by lying on the ground and using hands and feet to create the required number of points to the star. Ask them to create five-, six- and then seven-pointed stars.

**2.** In their star base groups, the children should sit in a circle. Supply each team with a ball of shiny white wool. The leader in each group should hold on to one end of the wool and toss the ball across the circle to another team member. He or she should hold on to the other end of the wool as it is stretched between them and toss the ball on to someone else in the circle. This should continue until there is a zigzag of shiny white wool creating the team's own particular star within the circle. Keep the star as taut as possible. Can the group now stand up and hold the star flat between them?

You could finish this game by asking the children to sit down again and reverse the whole procedure, to end up with one big ball of wool with no tangles. The first team to do this wins the game.

**3.** In star teams, organize a race in which each member of the team in turn has to run to a fixed point and collect part of a star, which they bring back for the others to assemble. To make the game more challenging, the pieces that they assemble could be made from a star cut into strange jigsaw shapes. Of course, this will need to be prepared beforehand. Alternatively, they could just collect stars, which they then have to arrange in a particular pattern for the team to complete the task.

**4.** Challenge the star teams to become various shapes suggested by some well-known constellations—for example, a bull, a hunter, a plough, a horse, a fish, a set of scales or a crab.

## Best foot forward

Introduce the story of God's promise to Abraham through the stars in the sky. The story can be found in Genesis 12:1–9. To set the scene, you will need the children to work in their star groups, which will all be part of Abraham's extended family that he took with him into the desert. Each group will need the following items:

○ A large piece of tarpaulin or a very large sheet
○ Four chairs
○ Some bamboo canes

Explain that everyone is now part of the group travelling with Abraham from his home in Ur thousands of years ago. They are travelling through the desert to an unknown land to make a new start. God has asked Abraham to leave his home and to trust him for every step of the way. Wherever they stop, they will need to set up their nomadic tents. For this reason, everything has to be carried with them on the journey.

Let each group decide who will carry the items and then arrange them in the four corners of your hall or meeting area. Everyone should start walking in the same direction around the rim of the hall. As they do so, the overall leader should describe the journey, encouraging them to act out what you are talking about. For example:

Walking through the desert every day was hard work *(they should trudge wearily through the sand)*.

In the day, the sun beat down upon them *(wipe the sweat from their faces and protect their eyes from the sun)*.

Sometimes the sand blew into their faces *(draw up an imaginary headdress over their eyes)*.

At night, it could be very cold *(shiver and wrap their arms about themselves tightly)*.

They had to keep a constant lookout for watering places for themselves and their animals *(looking around to the left and right for water)*.

When some grew weak, they helped each other to keep going *(some should help others to walk)*.

Sometimes they felt like giving up *(stand still, looking dejected)*.

But Abraham encouraged them to go on trusting God *(react to hearing his words and get going again)*.

At night, they camped under the stars.

At this last description, the group should come to a halt and make their desert tent from the chairs, bamboo and tarpaulin. Once they are all inside, turn down the lights or draw the curtains to darken the room. If you have fixed fluorescent stars around the walls and on the ceiling, these should now be visible and shining. If that hasn't been possible, you must help the children to imagine the stars in the sky, using the following words.

At night sometimes Abraham would look out across the sand and up into the night sky. *(The groups should crawl out of their tents, looking upwards.)* It was then that he felt very close to God and was sure that God was saying things to him about what would happen in the future. He felt God tell him that one day his family would become a great nation. It would be a family with faith in God, and the number of people in this family would be beyond counting. They would be more than the number of stars up in the sky.

As the children sit outside their tents, go on to tell them that Abraham had no children of his own so it seemed impossible for this promise from God to come true. However, he trusted that God would keep his promise. Whenever he looked up at the night sky on his journey, he took courage because he knew that God would not let him down.

And God did keep his promise because, when they eventually reached the new country, Abraham did have a miracle son in his old age. That son had children and those children had children and so on, generation after generation, until one day into that family was born Jesus, whose birth was signalled by a star in the sky. Now, the people who are part of the family of Jesus are all over the world. This family, down the years, has become so big that it is beyond counting. Its members are more than the stars we can see in the sky!

## Footrest

At this point in the programme, take a break for something to drink and eat. Those who finish quickly could use the time to continue decorating their star bases.

## Footprints

Now comes an opportunity for everyone to visit two or three workshops, depending on the time available, in which they can explore the theme of the feast further through drama ('Footlights'), music ('Footnotes') and craft ('Fancy footwork').

### Footlights

Begin this drama workshop with some simple activities to continue the theme of 'spotlighting the stars'. Ask the group to shuffle around the room anonymously and secretively. On the signal of 'lights, camera, action', they should freeze into statues representing various types of stars who are in the spotlight—becoming, for example, pop stars, sports stars, TV stars, or film stars. Now ask them out to act out these roles as extravagantly and ostentatiously as possible. Freeze them again after a while and ask someone to be an interviewer who has come to ask questions of these starlets—these should be fun questions about their lifestyle, their attitude to fame and riches, and their plans for the future. With younger children, have them mime out being these different types of stars in quick succession.

By contrast, the star of the Epiphany story went almost unnoticed by the world. Jesus' birth and early life were not in the spotlight of publicity and media attention. Even the wise men must have wondered if they were going to find anyone of any significance at the end of their long journey. Use this idea as a prompt for a piece of extempore drama with the children:

Remind the children briefly of the story of the wise men and then set the scene in an overnight camp where they and their servants have stopped on their journey west. What sorts of conversations were being held among the servants at night around the campfires? Split up into groups of four of five and ask them to come up with some possible conversations as they talk about what is happening. Each piece of impromptu drama should start with the words 'I wish they'd never seen that special star...' and end with the line: 'Look, the star up there is shining brighter than ever!'

*(Hints: they could talk about the discomforts of the journey, missing home, the strange new places they have visited on the way, the rumours of what the star is leading to, the way they are treated, even the bad temper of the camels.)*

Younger children could, with more guidance and direction, act out some of the ups and downs of the journey with the wise men. In many ways, this will echo the desert travels of Abraham already told, but this time the stars in the sky did not just point the way to a worldwide family of faith: the sky contained one particular star which was going to help the world discover how all that would happen. After each directed reenactment of part of the journey, link it up by having everyone say something like, 'But the star is still shining, so we must keep following.'

In addition to the earlier ideas, the children could act out the bumpy ride, the uncomfortable overnight conditions in the tents, coming across strange new places, the nervous feeling of being at the court of King Herod, the frantic search around the streets of Bethlehem, the shock at arriving at a poor peasant home and seeing a young child, the warning dream about their return, and their hurried journey back by a different way.

Either of these presentations could be rehearsed to become part of a presentation to show at the end of the programme.

## Footnotes

The story of the wise men is celebrated in a number of Christmas carols. In addition, the theme of light is picked up in a number of songs, such as:

Keep a light in your eyes (from *Big Blue Planet*)
We are marching in the light of God (*Kidsource* 350)
The Lord is my light (from *Many and Great*, Wild Goose)
The light of Christ (*Mission Praise* 652)

Two other songs that would fit the bill for this programme are 'He made the stars to shine' (*Junior Praise* 76) and 'Shine, Jesus, shine' (*Kidsource* 237), both of which lend themselves to actions that could add to the performance.

In the Old Testament we are told that God named all the stars that he created (Isaiah 40:26), and we also read that at the creation of the world the stars sang together (Job 38:7). Perhaps you could start this workshop by wondering about what sort of music singing stars would make and what it might sound like.

## Fancy footwork

Choose from the following star-themed crafts.

1. From the beginning of time, ancient civilizations have looked up at the stars and seen patterns in them, which they have named after people, animals and various objects. We know these patterns today as the constellations. Show pictures of some of them to the children and use this as a prompt to ask them to create their own constellations from a set of stars that they have. Each child needs about twelve small stick-on silver stars and a piece of black

card. Using only these items, they should create the outline of a new constellation of people, animals or objects from the stories they have heard today. Can they guess what shape each other's mysterious set of stars makes?

**2.** From craft shops, obtain some small star-shaped plain boxes, which the children can decorate to become special places in which to collect treasured items throughout the year ahead.

**3.** Star lampshades are a feature of festivals in many parts of the world, especially India. For each star lampshade, you will need five card copies of the template on page 226. Cut out each shape, adding some decoration. With a hole-punch, create a number of holes in each 'arm' of the star to let the light through. Fold along every dotted line and draw the sides together to make each section, fixing with glue, double-sided tape or a stapler. Finally, join together the five sections. This can be fiddly and it is best to work with a group or a partner. Younger children will need adult help.

**4.** Christmas and Epiphany are marked by various special stars around Europe. The Farol star is originally from Spain but is still used as part of a Filipino Christmas. You will need a wire coat-hanger, crêpe paper, scissors, glue, coloured paper and ribbon. Shape the wire hanger into a circle and wind the crêpe around the wire to decorate the circle. Cut out a large star from card and attach it with its five points touching the circle of the hanger. One point should be line with the hanger's hook, by which the star will be hung. Further decorate the star with circles of card behind each of its inner angles and add some ribbon tassles to the bottom two points of the star, opposite the hook at the top.

**5.** Another simple way to make stars is to use drinking straws. Form a triangle with three slightly overlapping straws, which you should then connect together where they cross over, either with glue or by making a hole with a punch through two straws and tying them together with cotton. Do the same with a second set of three straws, and then place the two triangles on top of each other to create the shape of a six-pointed star. Cover this frame with tissue paper to create a large star to hang. In addition, use smaller pieces of cut-up straws to create tiny stars in the same way and put them all together to make a star mobile.

There are other ideas for Epiphany crafts in the *Barnabas* books listed on page 232.


## Foothold

For the concluding time of reflection, you will need a four-pointed star cut in such a way that one of the points of the star is slightly elongated. You will need one star for each of the teams. On the back of each star, attach a simple cross, such as a palm cross. You will also need a pack of silver or gold stars for each team group and a circle of black felt for the centre of each team circle. Gather the children in team group circles, each with a leader. One overall leader should read the words below, while each team leader directs the actions that accompany them.

**Leader**: In the beginning, God made the stars in the sky. He named them and designed them to light up the darkness.

*Have each team arrange a series of stars on the black felt, one for each member of the team.*

**Leader**: These are the stars of creation. *(Pause)*
In the desert, God told Abraham to look up at the sky and promised him that one day his family of faith would be as many as the stars he could see.

Reproduced with permission from *Footsteps to the Feast* published by BRF 2007 (978 1 84101 464 7).

*The leader for each team should start counting the stars, but multiply numbers quite rapidly, counting like this: 1, 2, 3, 4, 5, 10, 100, 1000, 10000, 1 million!*

**Leader:** These are the stars of promise. *(Pause)*
One day, eastern astronomers looked up in the sky and saw a special star. They knew that it meant an important child had been born.

*The leader for each team should place the four-pointed star among the other stars.*

**Leader:** This is the star of the king. *(Pause)*
This star pointed to Jesus. The star also held a clue to the way that Jesus would defeat the darkness for everyone.

*The leader for each team should turn over the four-pointed star to reveal the cross hidden beneath it.*

**Leader:** This is the star of victory. *(Pause)*
The star shines out in every direction of the compass—north, south, east and west—drawing all peoples of the world to the love of God.

*Turn the star around again. The leaders should point to each compass point shown by the star.*

**Leader:** This is the star of a new beginning. *(Pause)*
As people are lit up by the light of Jesus, more and more are becoming part of the biggest family on earth.

Reproduced with permission from *Footsteps to the Feast* published by BRF 2007 (978 1 84101 464 7).

*The leaders should direct the teams to add more stars around the central star on the black felt—at least one new star for every child present.*

**Leader:** These are the stars of the kingdom. *(Pause)*
Those who point others to the way of God will shine like stars in the sky. Amen

## Footsteps to the feast

Use the Footsteps chant from today's session to walk everyone into a huge circle for a finale to the programme. Once in that circle, everyone should join hands and then follow instructions from a leader, who is going to help the circle turn into a great star. The following instructions for creating a six- pointed star are based on a circle of 25 people.

☉ Go around the circle numbering everybody 1, 2, 3 or 4.
☉ All those who are number 1 should stay rooted to the spot at the circumference of the circle.
☉ All those numbered 2 and 4 should take one step in towards the centre of the circle.
☉ All those numbered 3 should take two steps toward the centre of the circle.

Make sure hands are held the whole time. In this way (maybe with some slight adjustments), everyone should have created a six-pointed star together. To complete the effect of this human sculptured star, ask each person to link up with their neighbour not just by a simple handhold, but also by each becoming a star shape, so that they touch their neighbour with hands held high and feet splayed out, touching each other

Once the living star is in place, have the group repeat the star

Reproduced with permission from *Footsteps to the Feast* published by BRF 2007 (978 1 84101 464 7).

blessing below for the year ahead. The blessing is taken from Matthew 5:16.

> *Jesus says, 'Make your light shine, so that others will see the good that you do and will praise your Father in heaven.' Amen*

## Stepping out

Finish this Footsteps event by inviting others, such as parents and carers, to join you for a feast together. Include plenty of appropriate foodstuffs decorated with stars or baked in star shapes.

# 3

# Grandparents' day!

## A special event to celebrate the feast of Candlemas

The relationship between grandparents and grandchildren can be a very special one. It is almost always a proud moment for a grandad or granny when they hold their newborn grandchild for the first time. At its best, this special bond across the generations can play a vital role in helping a child to grow up into emotional and spiritual maturity.

Although Simeon and Anna in today's story are not related to Jesus by blood, they could be seen as his spiritual grandparents. They rejoice in his birth, for which they have long hoped, they foresee the special purposes of his life and they can't help but tell others of the news of his arrival. Proud grandparents, indeed!

Today's theme explores this story, and it would be a great opportunity to invite along the children's own grandparents, either to take part in the programme with their grandchildren or to be there at the end to join in the feast. However, sensitivity needs to be observed for those children who do not have grandparents to invite, for whatever reason.

### Bible footsteps

The story can be found in Luke 2:22–38.

# First steps

After a general welcome and introductions to the leader and team, introduce some feet-connected warm-up exercises with the children to emphasize the theme of *Footsteps to the feast*. For example, ask the group to start walking on the spot and then introduce different sorts of walking, such as walking uphill, walking downhill, walking very softly and quietly so that no one hears, walking with very tired feet, running, shuffling along in a crowd, rubbing their feet because they are sore, stretching their feet after a long day's journey. Make this as much fun as possible and end by asking the children to hide their feet by sitting on the floor cross-legged.

To introduce the theme, use some of the following questions with the group.

⊙ I wonder who has had a baby brother or sister recently? Who came to visit when the baby was born? Did you have a special party? Were special presents given? What were they and who gave them?

⊙ I wonder who has been to a special service in a church to say 'thank you' for a baby? Was it a christening? Or a dedication? Or a special thanksgiving? What happened? Who was there?

⊙ I wonder who has been to visit their grandparents recently? Does anyone have their grandparents living nearby? What sort of things do you do together? Are there things you can say and do with your grandparents that are special?

Today's *Footsteps to the feast* is about a family who wanted to say a special 'thank you' to God for the birth of their new baby. They travelled to the big city of Jerusalem and to the special big 'church' there called the temple. They brought a gift to say 'thank you'. At the special service, an elderly man and an elderly woman, who were a little like grandparents to the baby, had some special things to say, which the baby's parents never forgot.

## Footsteps chant

Here is a chant that you could teach the children, which they could use as they walk between the activities and between parts of the story. It acts as a rhythmic way to hold the day together. It works well if the leader calls out each line and the children echo. Find your own rhythm for doing this, and introduce clapping to help the movement along.

*We're following Bible footsteps*
*For our feast today.*
*A grandfather and grandmother*
*Had special things to say.*

## First footing

Introduce the story by telling it from Anna's perspective. This story is called 'Unstoppable Great-granny Anna'.

Most great-grannies, when they reach their 80s, are about ready to put their feet up, to take things more easily and let others do the rushing about—but not Anna! Oh, no!

Nothing seemed too much trouble for Anna. She was unstoppable. She was as busy serving God at 84 as she had been at 24. The temple in Jerusalem was the centre of her life. It wasn't just the services—morning and evening, rain or shine, she was always there, singing and praying as if fit to burst—but it was also true for all the day-to-day temple jobs.

She did the temple cleaning so well that no one ever had to use a dusty prayer book. *(Mime dusting)* She made the temple tea so well that no one ever went away thirsty. *(Mime sipping tea)* She welcomed people at the temple door so well that no one ever felt like a stranger. *(Mime welcoming)* She was always ready with a smile, a kind word for those who were lonely or a special prayer for those in trouble. They called her the prophetess—and, believe me, that was quite an honour in those days. Very few women had been given such a special title.

Yes, Great-granny Anna was unstoppable, but she also had a special secret. From time to time she shared it with those who were ready to listen. *(Mime sharing a secret)* You see, when she was praying, singing, welcoming, making the tea, cleaning and caring for others, she was also doing something else. She was on the lookout. *(Mime being on the lookout)* She was waiting for God's promised rescuer—the person who God had said would come to sort out the mess of this world. She was sure she was going to meet him one day, though time was ticking on for Anna.

It was a very ordinary morning when something most extraordinary happened. A young couple arrived with their six-week-old baby for a special 'thank you' service. Anna, as usual, was unstoppable, handing out the books, smiling at the worshippers and welcoming new visitors. But when she saw this couple and, in particular, this baby, she felt a little tingle of excitement. *(Mime a tingle)* When she went into the service to join with everyone for the celebration, she saw a most amazing thing.

The baby was being held by a friendly elderly man called Simeon. *(Mime holding the baby)* She knew him because he often visited the temple. He was younger than Anna but, even so, a grandad in his own right. But that wasn't the most remarkable thing. You see, this grandad was singing— a singing grandad! For once, the unstoppable Anna was stopped in her tracks. Grandad Simeon was singing about the baby.

*Now I can go in peace*
*And my long waiting cease.*
*God's rescuer has come,*
*A light for everyone.*

Anna gazed, open-mouthed. No wonder she had tingled when she saw this baby. *(Mime a tingle)* This baby was God's special rescuer, God's special light for the world. A baby! Of course! How like God to take them all by surprise.

Anna was so excited, she just had to tell everyone about it. She told the people who came to the temple doors. *(Mime telling people the news)* She told the people who drank her temple tea. *(Mime telling people over tea)* She told the people she prayed with on the temple steps *(Mime telling people while praying)* and she told the people with whom she cleaned and polished. *(Mime telling people while polishing)*

Because of Great-granny Anna, lots of people got to hear about Jesus. Anna was unstoppable and so, as it turned out, was Jesus—the light of the world.

## Footbridge

One of the following games can be used to create a bridge between the introduction to the story and a more in-depth exploration.

## Just a minute

Today's story is about a dedicated life of waiting for God's moment. Imagine waiting up to 84 years for your big moment of street evangelism! Play some waiting games with the children—for example, one in which the children have to guess whether a certain amount of time has elapsed. Have the children sit in a circle and ask them to stand up when they think a certain number of seconds have passed. Begin with short periods like 15, 20 or 40 seconds and then work up towards one minute or two (for older children). Who was closest each time?

## What's the time, Grandad Simeon?

This game is based on the traditional game 'What's the time, Mr Wolf?' The children need to creep up from a baseline towards Grandad Simeon, who is played by an adult leader. They call out 'What's the time, Grandad Simeon?' S/he gives various times but when s/he says 'It's dedication time', s/he should try to tag one of the children. Before s/he can do this, the children can try to run back to the baseline where they are safe.

## Fit or miss

Clearly, the years of watching and praying had prepared Simeon to recognize God's rescuer when he came, even though he was wrapped up as a baby. Simeon was able to see what God was doing when many others missed it. Beforehand, hide a series of items around the room in places that are not normal for those objects: for example, hide a cup not in the kitchen cupboard but down the back of the piano; place a spoon not in the cutlery drawer but balanced on top of a picture on the wall. Each time, send the children to look first of all in the obvious place for the item you mention, and then free them to go and look for it in an unusual place.

## What's my line?

Today's story is not only about the dedication of Jesus, but also the dedication of Anna and Simeon, who had given their lives to prayer and the service of others in the temple. Play a game of charades in which the children have one minute to act out an occupation that calls for lifelong dedication. The others should try to guess what that occupation is. Occupations could include doctor, nurse, fireman, research scientist, concert pianist, top athlete and vet. It would also be appropriate to include an opportunity for children to mime the jobs that their grandparents do or did, if they know what these are. Many older people will have been in the same job for most of their life.

# Best foot forward

In the four corners of the hall or church where you are holding the event, set up four focus areas to represent the four sections of the story. Using the chant that you have taught the children, march them to each corner. Pause there briefly as you tell part of the story in outline, ready for the group activities to follow. Perhaps four different leaders could prepare and tell each part of the story very briefly.

## Focus area 1

**Visual aid:** a baby doll in a Moses basket. (After you have told the story here, take the baby with you on the journey.)

**Story outline:** Mary and Joseph were so excited. They had been given the gift of a baby boy. Jesus was their miracle child, promised by God and named by his angels. After about six months, it was time to take the baby to Jerusalem, the capital of their country, to visit the temple for a special thanksgiving service. They wanted to offer their baby back to God, and dedicate him to God's service.

## Focus area 2

**Visual aid:** some packing cases arranged as the steps of the temple, with two large cardboard rolls on end, representing two of the temple pillars.

**Story outline:** Mary and Joseph arrived in the busy capital and made their way through the streets to the huge and impressive temple building. There were many steps to climb in order to reach the courts where they would have the special service for their child. It must have been very frightening and overwhelming for them, compared to the small village they had come from.

## Focus area 3

**Visual aid:** a man dressed in a long robe to represent Grandad Simeon. (You could ask one of the grandfathers linked to your children's group to play this role.)

**Story outline:** As the family was involved in the service, an elderly man arrived, looking for something or someone. When he saw the baby, his eyes lit up and, with permission from Mary, he took the baby into his arms and began to sing a song. He sang that this was God's special rescuer, come to bring hope to Israel and the whole world. He would be a light that would lighten up everyone's lives. He warned Mary, though, that her heart would one day be broken by what happened to this child, but also promised that many people would be rescued through him.

## Focus area 4

**Visual aid:** a woman in a long dress and shawl to represent Grandma Anna. (You could ask one of the grandmothers linked to your children's group to play this role.)

**Story outline:** Just after Simeon finished singing, a granny called Anna arrived. She, too, had been on the lookout for God's special rescuer and she became very excited when she heard Simeon's song and saw the baby Jesus. She began to rush around and tell everyone she met that God had kept his promise.

## Footrest

Time for a refreshment break. Have a drink and some biscuits ready for the children.

## Footprints

Divide the children into three groups. (It would be best to do this early in the session, when they are registered.) The grouping could be done by age, or each group could be a mixture of ages, which would allow for friends and brothers and sisters to stay together if they prefer. Each group will then visit each of the three following activities in turn, allowing about ten minutes for each one. Each activity works with the story creatively.

### Footlights

Choose one of the following drama games to explore the story creatively with the children. Depending on the ages of the children, the leader can use some or all of the following ideas.

**1.** Spend a moment identifying the different emotions and moods in the story you have just heard. Create statues of these emotions, which you then can contribute in a retelling of the story.

**2.** As a group, create a series of freeze-frames for different parts of the story—for example, Mary and Joseph with others and a donkey on the road to Jerusalem; Mary and Joseph and strangers on the steps of the temple; Mary and Joseph and worshippers at the service; Mary and Joseph and priests hearing Simeon sing his song; Mary and Joseph watching Anna tell everyone about Jesus. When each freeze-frame is ready, you could take a digital photograph and create a storyboard from the children's mimes. Alternatively, you could briefly interview the people in each frame and see what feelings and perspectives they have on the story of which they are now a part.

**3.** With older groups, it is fun to imagine other characters who must have been part of this story but are not mentioned in the Bible, such as fellow travellers, fellow worshippers and other friends and relatives of the main characters. Hot-seat these characters to investigate how they see the story and what happened.

**4.** As a group, act out the whole story with parts for Mary, Joseph, friends from Nazareth, Simeon, Anna and other worshippers.

## Footnotes

Have a range of instruments ready to create sounds for the story and to accompany any songs that you teach. Choose one of the following activities.

**1.** Begin by using a celebration song for the baby that has been born. Perhaps you could go back to a verse of a Christmas carol or maybe you could teach a simple lullaby (the sort of song Mary might have sung to baby Jesus to keep him from becoming restless on the long journey).

**2.** Using percussion instruments, recreate the sounds of the long walk to Jerusalem. There may have been other noises on the way apart from footsteps, such as the sound of the donkey's hooves on the stones.

**3.** Use wind instruments to create the more mysterious sound of the worship at the temple. You could sing together a song such as 'We have come into his house to worship him' (*Mission Praise* 729, verse 1 only).

**4.** Teach the group the Nunc Dimittis (the song of Simeon). There are various versions—for example, 'Faithful vigil ended' (*Psalm Praise* 30); 'Lord, now let your servant' (*Psalm Praise 31*); 'Let me now depart in peace' (*Psalm Praise* 32). Alternatively, use other songs on the theme of light, such as 'Keep me shining Lord' (*Junior Praise* 147); 'Lord, the light of your love is shining' (*Mission Praise* 445); 'Jesus bids us shine' (*Junior Praise* 128) or 'This little light of mine' (*Junior Praise* 258).

**5.** End on a celebratory song with musical accompaniment that picks up the joy Anna showed as she told others about Jesus. You could sing one verse of 'Go tell it on the mountain' (*Mission Praise* 179) plus the chorus.

## Fancy footwork

Choose from the following craft ideas according to the age range and experience of your group of children.

**1.** Make candleholders from modelling clay. These could be left on one side to dry and, at the end, taken home to be painted.

**2.** Make a Moses basket. A simple basket can be made by folding paper into a box shape using a simple box net and then gluing a handle to the finished basket. This could be painted and decorated. You could add some tissue paper 'straw' and a jelly bean baby.

**3.** Make candle pictures. Use coloured paper to create a mosaic, or cellophane or coloured acetate within a frame so that light can shine through your picture. Decorate and paint it.

## Foothold

Sit the children in one large circle or several smaller circles, each with an adult in charge. At the centre of each circle place a circular piece of white felt, with two tall pillar candles and a small tealight on top of the felt. Light the candles carefully and say that they represent the grandad and granny from our story—Simeon and Anna—and the baby Jesus.

Jesus is the light. He is the hope that had lit up Anna and Simeon's lives, and he will be the light for the whole world.

The candles can also represent two grandparents and a child. Encourage the children to pray for their grandparents. Whether the candles are tall or small, the same light of Jesus can burn as bright for both.

When the candles have been lit, use the simple concluding prayer below.

*Thank you, Jesus, that you came to be the light for grandparents and grandchildren, for young and old, for me and for those I love. Amen*

## Footsteps to the feast

This final game will take up a lot of space and is a fun way to conclude the session. Ask the children to stand in a huge circle, all holding hands. You could repeat the special chant for the day while they do this as quickly as they can (with some adult help).

You should all be facing inward. Explain that you want the circle to face outward, but without any of the children letting go of the hands they are holding. How will it be possible without twisting arms or getting into a contorted knot?

Explain how they are going to do it. Only you as leader will let go of the hand of the child to your left. Then you lead off, creating a circle within the outer circle, with the others following as soon as they feel themselves pulled into moving. The circle begins to wind in on itself.

Take care not to rush, because the end of the circle you are pulling will have to move faster than those on the inside. When you as leader have spiralled round and round as far as you can reasonably go, turn and begin to spiral out again, passing in between the coils you have created. Keep reminding everybody that they must not let go!

Gradually, as the circle unwinds following your lead, you all end up in a big circle again, but facing outward. Join hands with the child you originally let go of and reform the completed circle.

These stories have likewise turned people inside out, as they have followed in the footsteps of Jesus. Just like Simeon and Anna, people have seen new things and can now look out on to the world differently because they have spent time with these special stories from the Bible.

## Stepping out

Finish the session by having a selection of small cakes and biscuits to eat and juice to drink, which the children can enjoy in the circle(s) with parents and grandparents joining them. It would be good to encourage any grandparents who live nearby to bake or bring some cakes as a contribution to this feast.

After this, the children should collect the crafts they have made and then it is time to go home.

# 4

# Fast forward!

## A special event for the feast of Lent

The momentous and mysterious events celebrated at Easter are central to Christian belief. The great feast of Easter is so important that, in the early church, Easter became a popular time for baptisms. The period of instruction before baptism lasted for 40 days to reflect the time Jesus spent in the desert at the start of his ministry. This period of preparation has become the time that we call Lent.

During the six weeks of Lent, it became the custom for Christians to undertake some sort of personal self-discipline in order to have more time for prayer. Only in this way was it felt that the faithful would be really ready to enter into the wonder of what Jesus did on the cross for all people, for all time. Still today, this self-discipline can take various forms. Sometimes it involves fasting from certain foods and activities; sometimes it includes a pilgrimage or additional time set aside for quiet prayer or a retreat. Often Christians decide during Lent to read a recommended book or make the effort to join a six-week study course run by the local church.

This preparation for the mystery of Easter is still patterned on Jesus' own 40-day preparation for his ministry, which we can read about in the Gospels. After his baptism, Jesus went into the desert and fasted. He was getting ready for the work God had for him to do. It was a time when he had to make the choice about what sort of rescuer-king he was going to be. It involved some tough decisions as he faced other ways in which he was tempted to win back the world from the destructive effects of sin.

The story of Jesus' time in the desert and the temptations he faced provide the content for this *Footsteps to the Feast* programme for Lent. Through his fast, Jesus discovered how to move forward in God's way. The outline for this children's event explores what this 'fast forward' might mean for us, as well as helping children to get ready for the Easter feast that is drawing near.

## Bible footsteps

The story can be found in Matthew 4:1–11.

# First steps

After welcoming the children and introducing the team, move straight into some fun warm-up exercises that help set the scene for today's story. To pick up on the 'Fast forward!' idea, do one of the following activities.

1. Work through a typical morning's routine, incorporating ideas from the children, which can then be turned into an exaggerated mime. For example: wake up in the morning (stretching arms with a big yawn); wash (soap yourself in the shower); get dressed (put on clothes); run downstairs (quick steps on the spot); have breakfast (pour cereal and milk and eat it noisily); remember that today is the special 'Fast forward' event (a big cheer and a smile); clean teeth (exaggerated brushstrokes); watch some TV cartoons (in a seated position, laughing at an imaginary screen); pack a snack lunch (wrap up fruit and crisps and so on); walk or be driven to the event (walk on the spot or sit in a car, bobbing up and down and swerving left and right).

Go through these actions a few times and then try doing them faster: in other words, fast-forward the morning. You might also try to rewind the events, or even attempt a fast rewind, if you dare. Finally, go through the actions one last time but now leave out the breakfast, watching TV and the packed lunch. Instead, pull a face or rub your stomach in mock hunger. Today's 'Fast forward' involves someone missing out on food and other activities in order to give a bit more time to hearing God's voice.

**2.** A simpler alternative to this warm-up would be to use the commands 'fast forward', 'play', 'rewind' and 'pause' while you get the group doing various activities on the spot, such as running, hopping, walking, doing knee bends, jumping, heads-shoulders-knees-and-toes and so on. Set them off on one of these activities at a time but alter the pace or change direction with the commands. You could even turn it into a 'Simon says' game, where they should obey the command only if it is preceded by an appropriate 'Simon says' phrase.

Whichever warm-up you use, end by having the children sit down on the ground ready to be introduced to the theme.

## Footsteps chant

Here is a special chant that could be used throughout the session, both in between activities and as a way of drawing the children together for the next part of the programme. A leader should say each line and have the children repeat it, accompanied by a rhythmic clapping.

*We're travelling through a story*
*To find a mystery king.*
*Making footsteps to a feast,*
*What rescue will he bring?*

# First footing

Introduce the theme by asking the children to tell you their favourite sweets or snacks. Now ask them to imagine what it would be like if they had to go without these favourite foods for a while.

- ❂ I wonder if you would quickly get cross or moody?
- ❂ I wonder how long you could last without these foods?
- ❂ I wonder if, after a while, it would get easier and you might stop wanting these foods?
- ❂ I wonder if you think it might be good to have a break from your favourite foods?
- ❂ I wonder if you could use the money saved in another way?
- ❂ I wonder if this might be one way to discover what is really most important to you in life?

In today's story Jesus chose to go without food (this is known as 'fasting') for a long while. He needed extra time to think about what sort of rescuer-king he was going to be. History then, as now, is full of all sorts of great heroes and people who did brave and noble things to rescue others. Some used weapons and great armies; some used special skills or inventions; some used clever plans or attempted daring deeds. But what sort of hero was needed to rescue the world from the really big problems of selfishness, greed and pride? What sort of daring deed would defeat these enemies and give people real freedom? This is what Jesus was thinking about.

Jesus knew that God had sent him to save the world—his very name, Jesus, means 'the one who rescues'. But what sort of rescuer-king was he to be? When we have big questions to sort out, we often need time to think—time away from the ordinary routines of everyday life such as making meals, watching TV and having other chores to do. This is why Jesus went off into the desert.

- I wonder what sort of rescuer-king Jesus could be?
- I wonder what sort of rescuer-king others hoped Jesus would be?
- I wonder what sort of rescuer-king Jesus was tempted to be?

Tell the story of Jesus' time of testing in the desert. Involve the children by inviting them to copy certain actions and reactions. The storyteller uses the following outline.

Jesus decided he needed some time to be alone because he had big questions to sort out. He needed to decide what sort of rescuer-king God wanted him to be, so he went off into the desert. In the desert, there were rocks and sand to walk across. *(The children should walk on the spot, going slower and slower, stumbling over imaginary rocks)*

It was really hot during the day. *(Mime wiping sweat from foreheads and shielding eyes from the sun)*

It was very cold at night… *(Mime wrapping clothes around the body and shivering)* and there was very little to eat… *(Rub stomachs with hunger pains)* and almost nothing to drink. *(Pant with thirst and then imagine having a few drops of water from a water bottle to keep you going)*

Sometimes the wind blew the sand into his face and hands… *(Shield face from the stinging sand)* and it was easy to become confused and lose the way. *(Stand still, looking in all directions, confused)*

It was very lonely and quiet in the desert. *(Crouch down and look scared)* In this lonely, dangerous place Jesus wrestled with what sort of rescuer-king he was meant to be. *(Look puzzled)*

Once, he heard a menacing voice *(Put one hand to one ear,*

*listening)* that said:, 'Why don't you turn those stones over there into bread and give yourself something to eat?'

Jesus thought that using God's power in this way might certainly impress people, but would it really change their hearts? Jesus said, 'No!' *(Put up one hand firmly in a stop position in front of you)* He said, 'People need more than bread to be alive. They need all the words in God's book.'

Suddenly Jesus dreamed he was high on the top tower of the temple in Jerusalem. He heard the menacing voice again. *(One hand to one ear, listening)* 'Why don't you throw yourself down and see if God will send his angels to catch you before you hit the ground beneath?'

Jesus thought that using God's power in this way might certainly impress people, but would it really change their hearts? Jesus said, 'No!' *(Put one hand firmly in a stop position in front of you)* He said, 'There is no need to put God to the test like that.'

Finally, Jesus dreamt that he could see the whole world in one go. All its countries and kingdoms were beneath his feet. He heard the menacing voice again. *(Put one hand to one ear, listening)* 'If you serve me, I'll make you king of the entire world.'

Jesus thought that using God's power in this way would make him a king, but not the sort of king God wanted. This too would not change people's hearts. Jesus said, 'No!' *(Put one hand firmly in the stop position in front of you)* He said, 'I am to be a rescuer-king to show people how to love each other, not a worldly king to show people how to fight each other.'

After this, the voice went away. Jesus decided it was time

to begin his rescue work. He was now sure what sort of rescuer-king he had to be. He stretched out his arms wide to the left and the right and entrusted himself to God. *(Stretch out hands left and right in the form of a cross)*

I wonder what sort of rescuer-king Jesus was going to be?

End with the chant together (see above).

# Footbridge

Here are some suggestions for games you could play at this point in the programme.

## Can you resist?

Play this game in groups of four children. One child sits in a chair and must keep a straight face while the other three try different ways (using actions, pulling faces and saying different things) to make them smile or laugh. No touching is allowed. How long can each child in the group resist the temptation to laugh or smile? Give each child in the group a turn at being in the chair (as long as they want to do so).

## Freeze

This is a game for the whole group to play, using as wide a space as possible for the children to move about in. Set the children walking around (without knocking into each other). On command, they must freeze in one of the following three ways linked to the story.

- Stones (freeze curled up on the floor tightly like a ball)
- Towers (freeze stretching up as high as possible on tiptoes, reaching for the ceiling)

◎ Kings (freeze sitting on an imaginary throne, holding an imaginary orb in an open palm in one hand and an imaginary mace in the other)

Practise the commands a few times and then introduce another element. The children must hold the statue frozen in complete stillness for a count of 20 each time. Any movement means a child is counted 'out' and they then join the leaders to decide who will be out on the next round.

## Linked words

Divide the children into two or three groups and sit them in circles slightly away from each other, so that they cannot overhear what the other groups are saying. How many words associated with some key parts of the story can each circle come up with in a set time? Each child in the circle in turn should try to add a word to the list. Ask leaders to keep a record of how many words each circle contributes. Which team each time can find the most words linked to the key word?

Here are some possible key words: deserts, snack foods, bottled drinks, famous buildings, countries around the world.

## Crown the king

Divide the group into three or four teams. Create a 'desert' obstacle course using some of the following features.

◎ A large tray of small stones
◎ Two bowls on a plastic cloth (one containing a small amount of sand) and a plastic spoon
◎ A heavy piece of mat or canvas taped down on two sides, allowing it to become a tunnel through which to crawl
◎ A box of chocolates
◎ A stepladder (if possible, with steps up both sides)
◎ A large inflatable globe and a tennis racket

In addition, collect a set of items that might be worn by a king—for example, a special ring, a robe (colourful blanket), a crown (made of card or paper), an orb (a ball wrapped in gold paper), a mace (a bamboo stick wrapped in silver or gold paper), a throne (a chair with arms), a posh cushion, a colourful waistcoat, a pair of white gloves and so on.

Each member of the team must try to complete the obstacle course before he or she is allowed to bring one of the items back to base in order to dress a preselected team member as a king. The obstacle course will involve:

- Taking off socks and shoes and walking across the tray of stones before putting socks and shoes back on again.
- Using a plastic spoon to transfer the sand from one bowl to the other.
- Crawling through the mat or canvas tunnel.
- Opening up a chocolate sweet from the chocolate box, holding it on the hand without eating it for a count of 20, and then giving it to someone else.
- Climbing the ladder up to the top and back down again.
- Bouncing the inflatable globe ten times on the tennis racket without dropping it.

If the teams are larger than ten, speed up the game by stipulating that the next team member can start the obstacle course as soon as the previous person has finished and is on their way back with the item for the king. Which team will have its king dressed, crowned and seated on the throne first?

## Best foot forward

Set up four focus areas around the hall. Perhaps four teams could help create these areas at the beginning of the day while the children arrive. The four venues will help make visual the events in the story and give the children an opportunity to retell the story in their own words. Move the children between focus areas using the festival chant (see above), pausing for two or three minutes only at each venue.

**Focus area 1: the desert:** Borrow a small plastic swimming pool and fill it with some play sand and small stones. Give the children the opportunity to step into the sand and find the small stones, which they should collect together. Talk about the desert and its dangers. What sort of place would it be? Let the children tell you why they think Jesus chose to go into the desert.

**Focus area 2: the stones:** Take the stones collected from the last focus area and place them on to several paper plates at the second venue. If possible, arrange for a bright spotlight or sunlamp to be shining so that children can feel the heat of being in the desert. Ask them to imagine how hungry and thirsty people get in the desert. Let the children tell you about the first temptation that Jesus faced concerning the stones.

**Focus area 3: the temple:** Set up a tall stepladder or pile of stage blocks as high as you can safely go. Give the children an opportunity to stand on the top. (NB: for safety reasons, very young children should be accompanied or closely supervised.) Ask the children how it feels to be up so high. Were they to jump, would they be sure of landing safely? Let the children tell you about the second temptation that Jesus faced on top of the temple tower.

**Focus area 4: the world:** Lay a large map of the world on the ground (the Early Learning Centre has a large plastic world play mat for a game of Twister). Alternatively, arrange to have several globes that the children can pass around. Looking at the globes or down on to the world mat, what countries and parts of the world do the children recognize? What do they think God sees when he looks down on our world? What would you do about the world if you ruled over all the countries? Let the children tell you about the third temptation that Jesus faced, as he seemed to be on top of the world.

## Footrest

At this point in the programme, pause for a drink and a biscuit. If you dare (and this would be in keeping with the theme), why not offer only water to drink and bread cut into small circles like round stones to eat?

## Footprints

Divide the children into three groups. It will help to make these groups age-related as far as possible, so that the workshop leaders can pitch the drama, music and craft activities appropriately. Each group will spend approximately 10 minutes on each activity before moving on to the next one. Each group should have the opportunity to experience each workshop.

### Footlights

Begin this drama workshop with some warm-up activities in which the children have to imagine walking through the desert, picking up stones, climbing lots of stairs and lifting a huge world upon their shoulders like Atlas. After this, divide the children into four groups to act out the story. In each group, one person needs to be Jesus while the others are the voice of the tempter.

**Group 1: in the desert:** Jesus should mime walking in the desert and finding it hard. Each of the others should think up what to whisper to Jesus to make him feel like giving up and going home—

for example, 'It's going to be too hard', 'It will be lonely', 'No one will care', 'People don't want to be rescued' and so on. Let the children come up with their own ideas as well as actions to go along with what they say.

**Group 2: by the stones:** Jesus should mime how very hungry and thirsty he has become. The others should be ready to suggest all sorts of really tempting foods he could magic up to eat—the tastier and more exotic, the better. Again, let the children come up with the ideas and actions to go with the tempting foods. Jesus should decide when to interrupt with a firm 'No' and 'People need more than food to be really alive.'

**Group 3: on top of the temple:** Jesus should mime climbing up the temple steps and then standing—perhaps swaying slightly and a little dizzy—at the top. The others should be ready to persuade him to jump and trust that God will surely catch him, saying things like, 'He will send his angels', 'You'll be in the papers', 'People will admire you', 'You will be famous', 'People will be impressed and bound to become your followers'. Jesus should decide when to say 'No' and 'You don't need to put God to the test.'

**Group 4: on top of the world:** Jesus should be looking out amazed, as if he can see the whole world in one go. The others should be ready to tell him what a great king he would make, if only he rules their way—for example, 'Be cruel and tough', 'Be firm and unforgiving', 'Rule with a strong arm', 'Keep everyone under the thumb', 'Don't let anyone get away with anything', 'Use force' and so on. Again, Jesus should decide when to say 'No' and 'I'm not going to be that sort of king.'

Practise these activities and then put the whole scene together. One group could perform it later as part of a presentation at the end of the programme.

## Footnotes

For this music workshop, you will need a box of percussion instruments with enough for everyone in the group, so that they can create sound effects for the story.

- ☼ What sort of sound evokes the loneliness and vastness of the desert?
- ☼ What sort of sound evokes feelings of hunger and thirst?
- ☼ What sort of menacing sounds go with the voice of the tempter?
- ☼ What sort of sound evokes the strong 'No' that Jesus says each time he is tempted to be a different sort of rescuer-king?
- ☼ What sort of sound represents tempting foods, or climbing up to the top of the tower, or the whole world with all its people and cultures?

Small groups could work on creating each of these sound effects. Put them all together to create a sound-effect version of the story. Finally, draw the whole group together by learning a key song, which they could use later in a presentation. For example, you could use 'God's people aren't superbrave superheroes' or 'God so loved the world' (both by John Hardwick: see page 233 for details). Alternatively, you could take the song 'We have a king' (*Junior Praise* 264) and change the words to link with this story, as follows:

Verse 1: We have a king who needs no weapons… (x 3) And his name is Jesus.
Verse 2: We have a king who needs no magic… (x 3) And his name is Jesus.
Verse 3: We have a king who says 'no' to evil… (x 3) And his name is Jesus.
For the chorus, use the words 'Jesus, the king who rescues… (x 3) rescues everybody'.

## Fancy footwork

This three-dimensional picture of the story should be self-explanatory. It will help the children to remember the temptations that faced Jesus and the sort of king he eventually chose to become. You will need:

- An A4 piece of yellow or sand-coloured card
- Several small foot templates (cut from paper or carved into sliced vegetables for printing)
- Small pots of poster paint and paintbrushes or felt-tipped pens
- PVA glue
- Small bits of gravel
- Small pieces of balsa wood
- Some blue and some green Plasticine
- Gold card
- Garden twist

First of all, each child needs to print or stencil a series of winding footsteps across the piece of card, which represents the desert. At three points in the wandering of the feet, there will be the following three-dimensional features to represent the different temptations that came to Jesus:

1. In a patch of glue, stick a small pile of the gravel. Next to it, stick a piece of gold card cut in the shape of a tiny crown.
2. Glue together a small collection of balsa wood pieces to represent the temple and stick it next to the wandering footsteps. By the side, stick a piece of gold card cut in the shape of a tiny crown.
3. Roll a small ball of blue Plasticine and put some thin pieces of green on to it to create a tiny 'world'. Glue this also next to the wandering footprints and, by its side, a piece of gold card cut in the shape of a tiny crown.

4. Finally, at the end of the line of wandering footprints, stick another crown, but this time one made from the garden twist (to represent a small crown of thorns).

## Foothold

Using the chant for the day, gather the children into a number of small groups, each with a leader and sitting in a circle. In the middle of each group, place a circle of sand-coloured felt to represent the desert. On to the felt, put a golden crown cut from card and a wooden cross made from two small sticks tied together with twist. Encourage the children to be quiet as you use the following words in a final reflection on the whole programme.

Jesus went into the desert to decide the best way to be a rescuer-king. He could have used God's power to become a great ruler with a kingdom, armies and weapons. He could have used God's power to win people over in all sorts of dramatic and startling ways. But he chose to go God's way. He chose not to sit on a throne but to die on a cross. He chose not to wear a crown of gold but a crown of thorns. *(Pause)*

- ✪ I wonder why Jesus chose this way and said 'No' to the other ways of being a king?
- ✪ I wonder why Jesus thought this would really rescue people?
- ✪ I wonder why Jesus thought the other ways would not work?
- ✪ I wonder how this way of being a rescuer-king can really change the world?
- ✪ I wonder whether there are more important things in life than being well fed, being liked and having power?
- ✪ I wonder what this means for us on the way to Easter?

*(Pause)* End with the chant.

## Footsteps to the feast

To bring the programme to a close before you have some food together (a feast), you might use the following activity. If there are presentations and items to show parents and carers from the day, this could also be the point at which everything is brought together.

Stand in a circle with everyone's arms stretched out wide at shoulder height. Join up the circle with each left-hand palm on top of the next person's right-hand palm. Each child has now become the cross that Jesus was moving towards during the season of Lent—but that cross was to turn everything around.

The leader should now start a 'fast forward' movement by turning to his or her right to face outwards. As soon as he or she has done this and reconnected his/her right hand with the person now to the right, that person should likewise turn and thus set up a revolving cross-circle. This may need some practice, which should be fun and will neatly demonstrate the transformation that the cross brings to individuals and the world.

## Stepping out

Finish the session by having a selection of small cakes and biscuits to eat and juice to drink, which the children can enjoy in the circle(s) with parents and carers joining them.

After this, the children should collect the crafts they have made and then it is time to go home.

# 5

# The feast of feasts!

## A special event for Holy Week

The days that are the focus for this unit lead up to the 'feast of feasts' for Christians. They represent the high point of the story of salvation through Jesus Christ and are the heart of the mystery of God's love for his world. This is a week of Old Testament prophecy fulfilled, a week to which the Gospel writers devote a huge part of their stories of Jesus, and a week that takes those involved through the heights and depths of fear, hope and joy. Because this week is so important to Christians, it is marked by a whole host of special services, public processions and events. Nevertheless, many people outside the church are unaware of what this week means for Christians. For this reason, an increasing number of churches are organizing events to which they can invite children and families who do not normally come to Holy Week services, so that they can hear something of what Easter is really all about. The following outline is a two-hour programme for such an event.

### Bible footsteps

The story can be found in Matthew 21—28; Mark 11—16; Luke 19:28—24:53; John 12—20.

# First steps

So much happens in the Bible story of this week that there is no shortage of material to draw on. The following outline focuses on one event for each of the days, starting with Palm Sunday, as we follow the footsteps of Jesus through the drama of the week right up to and including the surprise of the first Easter morning. In order to do justice to these events, some of the stories are explored more deeply in the 'Footprints' sessions where the children work on drama, music and craft activities. It is important, however, not to give the impression that the days are disconnected from each other. To help with this, there are two suggested presentations in which the whole week is told as one continuous story.

## Festival chant

The following chant is designed to be used as you move through the story one day at a time. Learn the special words to a clapping rhythm by calling out each line and inviting the children to copy what you've said. Use this chant as you link the days in the story that follows and also as a connecting and attention-gathering signal throughout the event.

*We're on a special journey*
*Of footsteps to the feast.*
*We're travelling with Jesus:*
*The last, the lost, the least.*

*We're on a special journey*
*Of footsteps to the feast.*
*Jesus comes to rescue us:*
*The last, the lost, the least.*

# First footing

Welcome the children to this special day of stories and activities, introducing the leaders and making sure that everyone knows which group they are in and what will be happening where. It is really important on such days that children feel not only welcomed but also safe.

While children are arriving and being registered (if un-accompanied by parents for the event), they could decorate their group area with coloured feet. If there is time, they could also be invited to draw around their own feet on to a long roll of blank wallpaper to create a 'procession of feet' outlines, which could become a banner backcloth for the day.

Once all the children are gathered, use the theme of feet for a number of warm-up activities. For example, explain that we are all now on a journey to Jerusalem to discover the story of Easter. We are following Jesus' footsteps to a special feast or celebration. Ask them if their feet are ready to follow. Challenge the group to walk in various ways in small circles, where they are standing: on tiptoe, on their heels, on the sides of their feet, one foot in front of the other, standing on one foot and turning in a circle, using small jumps with their feet 'glued' together, linking toes and heels in a group of five and six children making a circle, hopping on one foot and then the other.

If there is time, continue this warm-up theme with similar ideas, such as practising having dancing feet or trying some 'Riverdance' footwork, skipping, or running on the spot, fast and then slow.

Today's event is a day of footsteps as we follow Jesus through eight days of drama—a drama that Christians believe changed the world. If you plan to use some group songs as part of the day (as well as those in the music workshop), this is a good time to bring them in, to help you begin to tell one of the stories that follow. Two songs you could use that help to lead into Palm Sunday are 'Clap your hands all you people' (*Junior Praise* 26) and 'We have a king who rides on a donkey' (*Junior Praise* 264). An alternative final verse could be 'How shall we show our love for Jesus? (x 3) Follow in his footsteps.'

Explain to the children that we are going to explore the week through stories and activities together. Excited feet soon become sore feet; tired feet become smelly feet; sad feet do eventually become dancing feet. This is the most amazing week ever! Set them thinking about the week to come with these open-ended questions:

- ☺ I wonder why this week is so special for Christians that they call it 'Holy Week'?
- ☺ I wonder why the Bible has so many stories about this one week?
- ☺ I wonder what it felt like to be there that week, following Jesus?
- ☺ I wonder what we will discover about Jesus and who he is as we follow the footsteps?

## Footbridge

Here are some simple games to play in groups, or with all the children together, to help you tell the story.

### Pigeons, palms and perfume

Stand the children in a circle and give each child the word pigeon, palm or perfume. Practise calling out one of these words, at which the children with that word should run across the circle and change places. Take the game further by inviting one or two children to stand in the middle and close up the circle. Now, when you call out one of the words, the children in the middle should use the opportunity provided by all the movement to find a place for themselves in the circle and so displace some others. Who'll be left in the middle? If you want all the children to move at any point, your signal word could be 'Footsteps'.

## Sound effects

The story of Palm Sunday is full of all sorts of actions and sounds. Divide the children into groups of three or four and give them different sounds and actions from the story of Palm Sunday—for example, cheering, waving, the clip-clop of a donkey, climbing trees, taking off coats, shouting 'Hosanna' and so on.

Now tell the story of Palm Sunday. Whenever you mention any of the different actions or sounds, the children should add in their contribution to the story. Try to repeat sounds or action cues as often as possible to catch them out.

## Four feet but three legs

Play a game in which teams have to collect various items from one end of the room in order to set up a Passover feast. Each team should have an even number of members because they must go in pairs, tied at the ankle, to negotiate a simple obstacle course and bring back what they need for their feast.

Set out a number of cones as obstacles. The children must weave in and out of the cones to reach the objects they are collecting at the other end. The objects needed could include a bread roll, a tablecloth, a bottle of red-coloured drink, paper plates, a towel, a basin, plastic cups, plastic cutlery, a jug and a large serving dish. The first team to collect a full set and lay out everything ready for the meal wins the game.

## Feet firmly on the ground

Organize the children into groups of five or six and then issue a series of challenges that involve feet on the ground. The children must find a way of linking up with each other (and not touching or leaning on any other object or person outside the group) in such a way that they have only a certain number of feet on the ground. Challenge them to do this with only five feet, then four feet, then three feet and perhaps only two feet touching the ground. They may not touch the ground with any other parts of their body.

## Best foot forward

This is a simple action-based story for the whole of Holy Week, which you could present while the children are all together. It will help them get ready for the different activities that they explore later. In between each of the days, use the festival chant that they have learnt to move the story on. Here are the actions for each day:

Palm Day:      wave hands high with fingers splayed.

Pigeon Day:    link thumbs and flap the other fingers to represent the wings of a bird.

Perfume Day:   waft hands towards your nose as if catching a beautiful smell.

Parable Day:   put one finger in front of your lips to call for silence and careful listening (to a story).

Passover Day:  pretend to eat and drink with your hands.

Painful Day:   point with the index finger to each wrist, one at a time (this is sign language for Jesus). Alternatively, put hands in front of face because you're not able to look at something terrible.

Prayerful Day: put hands together in prayer.

Promised Day:  hold out hands wide in excitement, because a miracle has happened.

For each day, the children should demonstrate the action as you very briefly tell what happened.

**Palm Day:** The week began with the crowds cheering and waving palm branches as Jesus came into Jerusalem. They were hoping he would be a new king but, to their surprise, he was riding on a donkey. He was going to be king, but not the sort of king they expected.

**Pigeon Day:** Soon after this, Jesus visited the temple and was angry at how it had become a market place. People were even buying and selling pigeons. It should have been a place of prayer. He pushed over the tables and the pigeons flew everywhere.

**Perfume Day:** In the evenings, Jesus spent time with his friends outside the city. At one meal, Mary came and poured perfume on to his feet to show how much she loved him. It was expensive perfume and some people were angry at the waste, but Jesus said that she was preparing him for his death. The smell of the perfume filled the whole place.

**Parable Day:** Each day at the temple Jesus would tell stories. He was such a wonderful storyteller that people listened intently, but they didn't always understand what he was saying. These were special stories called 'parables', which were meant to help people discover truths for themselves and help them draw closer to God.

**Passover Day:** On the Thursday of that week, Jesus went with his friends to an upstairs room in the back streets of the city for a special meal. They were remembering how God had rescued them long ago. Jesus broke bread and poured out wine and told his friends to do this to remember him in future, because now he too was about to rescue them. They were very puzzled.

**Painful Day:** That night, in a garden, Jesus was arrested and put on trial. People said terrible things about him, and early the next day they were taking him outside the city to kill him. They nailed him to a cross and by the afternoon he was dead. No one expected this to happen. It was a sad day but, strangely, it is called Good Friday.

**Prayerful Day:** Next day, Saturday, it seemed as if everything stood still. Jesus' friends were shocked and frightened. Had he let them down? All they could do was hope and pray.

**Promised Day:** Early in the morning on Sunday, some women went to the tomb, which was a cave in a garden—but the stone had been rolled away. They saw angels who told them that Jesus was alive, and later they saw him for themselves. Jesus was king, after all—a different sort of king who had beaten death and who could now be with everyone, everywhere, for ever.

## Footrest

Make time for a drink and a biscuit for the children before the next stage of the journey.

## Footprints

Arrange the next set of activities so that each group has an opportunity to experience a session working on drama activities ('Footlights'), craft ('Fancy footwork') and a music and dance activity ('Footnotes').

### Footlights

This suggested outline for a drama activity focuses on the 'smelly feet' aspect of the week! Begin with some warm-up games. For example:

1. Ask the children to walk around the room pretending that they are walking on different surfaces, such as on a pebbly beach, through drifting snow, across jagged rocks, on thin ice and over hot coals.

2. Now organize the children into pairs to try to illustrate the following foot words: footstool, footbridge, a game of football, and footpath.

3. Divide the group in two to work on two stories from Holy Week. Have one leader with each group and the story on a card. The leader should first read the story through to the children. The two stories involve 'smelly feet' being perfumed or washed. The stories are the woman with the perfume (Mark 14:3–9; John 12:1–3) and the last supper (John 13:1–14).

In each of the stories there is a common scene to mime (people reclining at a table, low to the ground, to have a meal) and then various activities. Choose someone to be Jesus and the woman in the first story and Jesus and Peter, in particular, in the second story. Each of the groups should work on how they will enact their drama without words; then they must decide at which point they are going to freeze the story like a photograph to show the other group.

Give time for the groups to work on the mime before they present their mime drama and freeze-frame. Once the drama is frozen at their chosen point, invite someone from the other group to come and interview the characters in role and see what they think about what has happened. Here are some questions to help prompt that interview process.

- What were the guests thinking as the woman poured all that perfume out?
- What was she feeling when she arrived at the meal?
- Why was Judas so angry?
- What do the people think about the way Jesus started talking about his death?
- What were the disciples thinking as they watched Jesus get ready to wash their feet?
- What might each of them have said as Jesus got closer to *their* feet?
- What was going on in Peter's mind?
- Why was Peter so indignant about having his feet washed?
- What did they think when Jesus said that unless he washed their feet, they couldn't belong to him?
- Why do you think Jesus did this so near to the time of his death?

An alternative piece of drama for younger children could be based on 'scurrying feet' in the temple, when Jesus caused such commotion there on 'Pigeon Day'. For this, divide the children into three groups, each around a low table. Each group plays one of the types of sellers in the marketplace of the temple. They each have their special 'group shout', so that, as it is built up, the temple becomes a noisier and noisier place. Here are the three selling shouts (add some appropriate actions to make this more fun):

⊕ Sheep, sheep, two for the price of one!
⊕ Pigeons, pigeons, get your pigeons here!
⊕ Money, money, change your money now!

The leader, as a narrator, should build up the drama of the scene as each selling chorus is added and grows louder. One of the children or a leader should be Jesus, who will end the commotion by shouting loudly, 'Stop! This is meant to be a house of prayer!'

At this point, 'Jesus' should rush over and tip up each table (take care!), scattering each of the groups. They should then freeze in a moment of shock and surprise. Appoint someone to be the interviewer who comes and asks each person what they think has happened. What do they think of Jesus? What sort of king does he think he is?

## Footnotes

For the music workshop, focus on some of the songs that tell the story of Easter and, in particular, Easter morning. There is a large repertoire to choose from. For example:

God's not dead, he is alive (*Junior Praise* 60)
He made the stars to shine (*Junior Praise* 76)
Jesus Christ is alive today (*Junior Praise* 129)
There is a green hill far away (*Junior Praise* 245)
Were you there when they crucified my Lord? (*Junior Praise* 269)
Led like a lamb to the slaughter (*Mission Praise* 402)
I'm special (*Mission Praise* 325)
From heaven you came (*Mission Praise* 162)

Whichever song you choose, first talk through with the group what sort of rhythms and accompanying musical instruments would best express the moods of the song. Choose instruments carefully, especially where there is a story to tell. Once the music and words are beginning to be known, suggest that the group work out some simple dance movements or actions to accompany the song for performance.

## Fancy footwork

Choose from the following craft ideas. There are more in *Easter Make & Do* published by BRF under the *Barnabas* imprint.

**1.** Prepare beforehand some simple outline pictures on pieces of clear acetate that combine both the open tomb at the foot of a hill and the three crosses on the top. The tomb should be surrounded by flowers and trees. Using acrylic paints in the manner of silk painting, ask the children to decorate their own individual pictures, adding the words 'Jesus is alive'. When hung up against a window, these pictures will let the light shine through like a piece of stained glass.

**2.** There are a number of craft ideas for reproducing different sorts of crosses in *A-cross the World* published by BRF under the *Barnabas* imprint. One suggestion is to make a very large cross to which all the children contribute. The Taizé cross, also in *A-cross the World*, would be suitable for this activity. It is made up of pictures and faces of people from around the world, which, if possible, should include pictures of the children on the event, perhaps using some digital prints or Polaroid images taken at some stage earlier and cut up appropriately for this craft.

**3.** Make an Easter story spiral by cutting out two circles of mediumweight card for each child. Cut a window opening near the edge of one circle, leaving a border above the opening so that the circle is not broken. Divide the other card circle into sections of the same size as the open window in the top circle. Draw a picture about an event of Holy Week in each section—for example, Palm Sunday (palm leaves), Jesus in the temple (pigeons), the last supper (bread and wine), Good Friday (a cross) and Easter Day (an empty tomb). Join the two card circles together through the middle with a split-pin fastener. Rest the window in the top circle over the first picture. As the top circle turns, it will reveal what happened on Jesus' journey.

**4.** Make up a calendar of this special Holy Week from an A3 sheet of card for each child. Divide it into eight squares, labelled with the different names of the days. In each of the squares, children should attach and decorate a series of items linked to the days. The items suggested are (in the order of the days followed at this event) a leaf, a feather, some scented paper, the opening lines of one of Jesus' parables on gold paper, a piece of matzo for the Passover, a small cross made with two long headless matchsticks, a closed double door with some cotton tied around two split-pin heads for door handles, and a shiny yellow paper circle to represent the sun rising on resurrection morning.

## Foothold

To bring the whole event together in a brief act of reflection and prayer, set out, on the floor of your hall or meeting area, a large equal-armed cross formed by a long piece of coloured rope, so that it fills up as much space as possible. Ask the children to come and stand around the perimeter of this cross.

Explain that they are going to reenact the whole week in one brief moment. All should turn and face in the same direction. On a signal from the leader, they should begin to walk slowly around the sides of the cross to the words of the chant that they have been using during the day. Slowly bring down the volume of the chant so that it gets quieter and quieter until it stops altogether. Continue to walk more and more slowly in silence, until eventually the children get back to the point at which they started their walk around the cross. Invite them to sit down.

Explain that they have been following Jesus on his way to the cross. It started with lots of noise, but ended in silence and sadness on Good Friday. Set the children thinking about this day with a few simple questions, but not necessarily asking for their response.

⚙ I wonder how Jesus' friends felt at the end of Good Friday?
⚙ I wonder where they felt it had all gone wrong?
⚙ I wonder why Jesus had to die?
⚙ I wonder how Jesus knew that he had to be hurt in this way and had to suffer like he did?

Christians believe that this day had to happen because God cares so much about us and he doesn't want us to face pain alone. Jesus, God's own dear Son, came to experience the worst of anything we might go through and to be right there with us.

Now, at each arm of the cross, under guidance from a leader, a candle should be lit. As each candle is lit, lead the children to think about different people who are facing hard times. For example:

⚙ People who feel lonely (just as Jesus was alone on the cross)
⚙ People who are hurting because of the way others have treated them (just as Jesus felt deserted on the cross)
⚙ People who are facing death (just as Jesus was on the cross)
⚙ People who are sad because of what has happened to them (just as Jesus was)

After each thought, and as the candle burns, the children should repeat the words, 'Jesus understands.' After a short pause, the candles should all be blown out when you say, 'And Jesus died.'

Now invite the children to stand up as you say:

But on the third day Jesus rose from the dead. There was a great crash of thunder. *(Ask the children to clap their hands together loudly)*

The stone was rolled away. *(Ask everyone to make a great crashing sound)*

Jesus was back from the dead. *(Everyone lift their hands on high)*

Women ran to the tomb. *(Run on the spot)*

They saw that Jesus was alive. *(Jump up and down and cheer)*

They ran to tell others the good news. *(Run on the spot again)*

End by teaching the Easter response: 'He is risen! He is risen indeed, hallelujah!' Finally, encourage loud applause and then go back to the festival chant for one last time.

## Footsteps to the feast

At the end of the event, once everything has been sorted and collected and announcements given, you could use this special circle game to finish.

### A Mexican wave of celebration

The children should hold hands in a huge circle. On instructions from the leader, everyone march inwards four steps and then backwards four steps as the festival chant is reused. All pause and hold out their hands wide so that everyone is holding on to each other in cross shapes, and say the words, 'Jesus died.'

Next, everyone should lift up hands (still holding on to each other) so that the circle becomes like a big crown, saying the words, 'Jesus is alive!' Finally, the hallelujah celebration should be a Mexican wave, started by the leader moving his or her right hand down and then up again. As soon as the person next to the leader feels their hand going up and down, they should do the same with their other hand and pass the wave along, to a repeated 'Hallelujah!'

## Stepping out

If possible, end the event with some refreshments. Invite parents and carers (if they are not already with you) so that they can join in the celebration and see what the children have been doing. An ideal food for this event would be hot cross buns.

# 6

# Can do day!

## A special event for the feast of Pentecost

Pentecost is sometimes described as the birthday of the Church. It was the day when the first followers of Jesus received the gift of the Holy Spirit. Jesus sent 'another comforter' just as he had promised, who would live inside them and make Jesus real to them. Through the Holy Spirit, Jesus could be with everyone, everywhere, anytime.

The Holy Spirit created a new body for Christ, made up of all who believe. This body is the Church, both local and worldwide. However, the gift of the Holy Spirit at Pentecost wasn't just a way of beginning the Church. The Spirit came with the sounds and signs of new energy and power. A great wind shook the place where the disciples were; flames of fire settled on their heads and they found they could speak God's praises in languages that they had never learned. This meant that the visitors to Jerusalem from all around the Mediterranean could understand what they were saying.

Pentecost enabled God's men and women to attempt and accomplish more than they ever thought possible. The Holy Spirit transformed them from a bunch of rather frightened and confused followers into a bold and gifted workforce for God. What they would have found impossible before that day suddenly became possible. It was no longer a case of 'I can't', but 'I can', through the inspiration of the Holy Spirit. Pentecost is the Christians' 'can do' day—and the same gift, the Holy Spirit, still enables his followers today.

The Holy Spirit is God invisibly at work in the world, equipping, renewing and empowering God's people. His work is as varied as the people he works through, so the Bible has many images for the life-giving Spirit of God. In the following programme there is an opportunity to explore some of the symbols and signs of the Spirit as well as to explore and celebrate the events of the first Pentecost—'can do' day—and relate them to life in the 21st century.

## Bible footsteps

The story can be found in Acts 2:1–42.

## First steps

Pentecost as described in Acts 2 occurred at the Jewish festival of Shavuot, which was the first of two harvest festivals in the Israeli agricultural year. It happened 50 days after Passover (hence the name Pentecost, which is derived from the Greek word for 50) and it was also a time when Jews celebrated the giving of the Ten Commandments on tablets of stone through Moses at Mount Sinai. Christians celebrate the day as the moment when God wrote his new laws of love on the tablets of our hearts by the gift of his Holy Spirit.

You could capture the atmosphere of a birthday celebration by decorating your meeting place with balloons, banners and streamers, as if for a birthday party. Tie together orange, yellow and red balloons to give the effect of flames. You may also consider putting up other images around the room that link to the different ways in which the Spirit of God is experienced and symbolized by the Church. These images would include outlines of a dove, jars of oil, something to illustrate the outpouring of water (perhaps a waterfall picture), images of the wind affecting the scenery, words of praise in various languages, and flames.

Here are some words of praise in a variety of languages that you could display. They all mean 'Praise the Lord'.

*Praise the Lord*
*Louez le Seigneur* (French)
*Loben Sie den Herrn* (German)
*Bwana Asifiwe* (Swahili)
*Stutu Hoos Prabhu* (Hindi)
*Siakudumisa* (from South Africa)
*Gloria al Senor* (Spanish)
*Khuda Acha Ate* (Urdu)

## Footsteps chant

Teach a chant for this special event which goes to a simple rhythmic clapping as the children echo each line back to the leader. Use the chant as a way of signalling the move from one part of the programme to another.

> *We're on a special journey,*
> *It's a story from God's book.*
> *There's wind and fire and words of praise,*
> *Let's take a second look.*

## First footing

Once you have welcomed the children, invite them to be involved in an active warm-up session for the event to get them ready for the story of Pentecost. The disciples in the upper room on that day had already been through a wide range of emotions and experiences to bring them to this point. They were probably exhausted as well as excited as they waited in that room. Take the children through a series of energetic mime activities to remind them of the events leading up to Pentecost. For example:

- Running on the spot (some of the disciples ran to the empty tomb on Easter morning when the women brought the news that Jesus was alive again).
- Running backwards in slow motion (as the disciples ran back to Jerusalem, wondering what would happen next).
- Curling up into a small ball (as the disciples waited in the upper room on that Easter Sunday afternoon).
- Jumping up suddenly with shock (as Jesus appeared to the disciples in the evening).
- Running around in small circles (as the disciples shared with each other what had taken place).
- Creeping through the streets of Jerusalem (because the disciples were still wary of the Jewish and Roman authorities, which had so recently condemned Jesus to death).
- Walking on the road to a nearby town and then jumping with excitement (as the disciples discovered that Jesus was suddenly with them).
- Fishing in the Sea of Galilee and then jumping with surprise (as the disciples discovered that Jesus was suddenly there too).
- Climbing the hill outside Jerusalem and then jumping up with surprise (as the disciples saw Jesus standing among them).
- Looking upwards in shock (as the disciples watched Jesus disappear for the last time and saw angels speaking to them).
- Skipping back to Jerusalem (as the disciples returned to wait, excited and amazed).
- Raising hands high in the air (as the disciples prayed together).
- Turning and pointing at everyone else as quickly as possible (as the disciples saw their numbers grow in that upper room and chose a new person to replace Judas).
- Sitting down quickly, ready for what would happen next (as the disciples waited for God's promise).

Finish the warm-up by asking the following questions:

- I wonder if these disciples had any idea of what was going to happen next?
- I wonder if they thought that Jesus would come back again, looking just like he did before?
- I wonder what the neighbours in the nearby houses thought as they saw the crowds coming and going in that upper room?
- I wonder what they talked about as they got ready for the next stage in God's rescue plan for the world?
- I wonder if some of them doubted that Jesus would come back and give them 'power from on high' as he had promised?
- I wonder who, apart from the disciples, was in the upper room? The story says that 120 people gathered there. Just who were they all?

## Footbridge

Here's a selection of Pentecost theme games, which you could use at this stage of the programme.

1. Christians believe that the Holy Spirit gives them new 'can-do' energy from God. To illustrate this in a fun way, ask the children to move around the room in different styles as if they were toys operated by battery. When you give the signal 'running down', they should begin to slow down gradually, coming to an eventual standstill like a battery-operated toy that no longer works. When you give the second signal, 'new life', they should start up again.

Try this as a number of different toys: for example, a battery operated rabbit, a dancing ballerina, a marching soldier and so on.

2. In groups of two or more children, create models of various machines that need power to make them run—for example, a washing machine, vacuum cleaner, lawn mower, windmill, and car. Again, at the signal 'switch off', they should freeze in the position of the machine with no movement; on the second signal, 'power

on', they should begin working again. This illustrates that just as machines need new power to make them function, so human beings need new power from God to be truly alive.

**3.** Play a traditional 'fruit salad' type of game, giving everyone in a circle one of the following three words: wind, flame or words. When you call out one of these words, the children with that word should cross the circle quickly to the other side, without knocking into anybody. You could then ask for some volunteers to be in the middle who, as everyone is moving, have to find a place in the circle, thus ousting others to be in the middle. If you want everyone to move at any point, you use the word 'Pentecost'.

**4.** Finally, ask the children to get into pairs and decide who is going to be the sculptor and who will become the sculpture. The sculpture must stand still like a lump of clay, wood, stone or marble. The sculptor will, with their partner's cooperation, arrange how that person will become a statue of something. In this case, the statue should first be of someone who has run out of energy. After a short while, freeze the sculpture and ask the sculptors to stand back so that everyone's masterpiece can be admired.

Now reverse the roles, so that the first sculptor becomes the sculpture. This time, the sculpture is to be of someone full of energy. Again, give time to view the sculpture gallery. This is a small illustration of what is happening at Pentecost to the disciples, as God empowers his people to be full of energy through the Holy Spirit.

You could link this activity to Paul's prayer in Ephesians 3:14–16, 21: 'I kneel in prayer to the Father. All beings in heaven and on earth receive their life from him. God is wonderful and glorious. I pray that his Spirit will make you become strong followers... His power at work in us can do far more than we dare ask or imagine.'

# Best foot forward

Pentecost is an event full of strange and unexpected sounds. Involve the children as you tell the story by asking them to provide sound effects and actions to accompany certain words, which you will include in the telling of the story. Here are the sounds and actions that go with the key words.

**Pentecost:** Jump up and do a celebratory dance, shouting 'Hooray, hooray!'

**Upper room:** Clap hands (as the door slams shut) and sit down quietly on the floor.

**Flames of fire:** Put both hands together in a prayer position above your head and make them flicker like a candle.

**Wind:** Make loud shushing noises as you stand swaying back and forth.

**Languages:** Shout out, with hands in the air, words such as 'Praise the Lord', 'Hallelujah', and 'Glory to God'.

**The crowds:** Raise both shoulders and hands as if puzzled and say 'What's up?'

**Drunk:** Hiccup a few times.

**Holy Spirit:** Whenever this is mentioned, choose a mixture of flame, wind and languages sounds and movements.

Now tell the story, making sure you repeat the above words as often as possible. End with the line, 'And the disciples from that upper room would never be the same again.'

Here's another version of the Pentecost story written by a member of our *Barnabas* ministry team, Lucy Moore. It involves saying the phrase 'but wonderful' whenever the leader says the word 'weird'. Pentecost was indeed a 'weird but wonderful' day, when everything changed.

Have you ever thought what weird but wonderful things God does for us? I need reminding that what he does is not only weird but wonderful too. So can you remind me? In this story, every time I say 'weird', can you say 'but wonderful'? I think that would be really weird *(but wonderful)*. You're right!

What a weird *(but wonderful)* time it was! We'd followed Jesus and seen him do things that were weird *(but wonderful)*. We'd watched him get arrested and die on the cross. Then there was that weird *(but wonderful)* first Sunday when he came back to life! After a picnic on the beach, which was weird *(but wonderful)*, Jesus took us up a hill outside the city here, and he said goodbye, promising he would be with us always. What a weird *(but wonderful)* thing to say when he just... disappeared!

So we kept meeting together to try to work out what weird *(but wonderful)* thing was going to happen next. And about a week after Jesus had left us, something weird *(but wonderful)* did happen!

We were all in a room in Jerusalem, when suddenly there was this weird *(but wonderful)* noise, like a rushing wind. It was coming from heaven, and the noise filled the whole house. Filled each of us up too—it was like we were floppy balloons being filled with air! Weird *(but wonderful)*!

And then we saw with our own eyes what looked like flames resting on each one of us. Weird *(but wonderful)*.

And we were all filled with the Holy Spirit, and we started speaking in languages we didn't know we could speak. Weird *(but wonderful)*.

And people from different countries in the street heard

us and were amazed that they could understand what we were saying. Some said we were drunk. Others said 'Weird' *(but wonderful)*.

Then Peter got up and told everyone that this was God's Holy Spirit at work, helping us all to have Jesus alive in us—and the crowds believed him. And do you know, about three thousand people became Christians that very day and the Church was born. And the same Holy Spirit helps us to have Jesus alive in us today! Weird *(but wonderful)*. Yes, you're absolutely right!

## Footrest

This is a moment to have a short break for the children and leaders, providing drinks and biscuits in groups.

## Footprints

Divide the children into three groups. (It would be best to do this early in the session, when they are registered.) The grouping could be done by age, or each group could be a mixture of ages, which would allow for friends and brothers and sisters to stay together if they prefer. Each group will then visit each of the three following activities in turn, allowing about ten minutes for each one. Each activity works with the story creatively.

## Footlights

1. Introduce a short drama workshop by rehearsing some of the emotions and feelings involved on the day of Pentecost. You could do this through a game in which you ask the children to stand in a

circle facing outwards. On the count of three and the word 'in', they should jump to face inwards, becoming a statue of someone with the different feelings and emotions of that day. Remind them that statues don't move or speak. Give a moment each time for the children to think how best to illustrate the feelings involved, which may include worry, fear, shock, excitement, puzzlement or happiness.

**2.** There are a lot of characters in this story and it would be fun to try to get into the feelings of the people who were there. Place a chair in the middle of the circle and invite the children to decide on different people who would have been either in the upstairs room or among the crowds. Ask for a volunteer (be ready to do it yourself first) who should then become one of the people suggested. He or she sits on the chair and the others can ask them questions about what they think was going on that day. Choose some unlikely visitors or passers-by as well as those sympathetic to the disciples.

**3.** Here is a short sketch about the meaning of Pentecost, written by *Barnabas* team member Lucy Moore, which could be rehearsed in the workshop for a presentation later. It builds on the idea of running out of energy or battery power in the games described above (see 'Footbridge' section).

**Narr 1:** Oh dear.

**All:** Something's not right.

**Narr 2:** Run down?

*Actors run on the spot, full of energy at first, but then getting tired.*

**Narr 3:** Worn out?

*Actors totter round like clockwork animals, full of energy at first, but gradually slowing down and stopping in funny postures.*

Reproduced with permission from *Footsteps to the Feast* published by BRF 2007 (978 1 84101 464 7).

**Narr 4:** Out of juice?

*Actors hold hands and pass along an electric shock that dwindles and stops, leaving the actors drooping.*

**Narr 5:** Out of puff?

*Actors turn into windmills whirring, which fizzle to a standstill.*

**Narr 6:** Lost the spark?

*Actors explode like fireworks, then fizzle out.*

**Narr 7:** Oh dear.
**All:** Something needs to change.
**Narr 1:** Jesus' disciples were waiting, quietly, calmly, praying to God, when suddenly there was a sound like a roaring wind.

*Actors look up in astonishment.*

**Narr 1:** And something like flames appeared over their heads.

*Actors point in surprise.*

**Narr 1:** And all of them were filled with the Holy Spirit.

*Actors jump up.*

**Narr 2:** What was run down... charged up *(running on the spot)*

**Narr 3:** What was worn out... became new *(like clockwork toys)*

**Narr 4:** What was out of juice… sparked to life *(like the electric fence)*

**Narr 5:** What was out of puff… got the wind in its sails *(like the windmills)*

**Narr 6:** What was dead and cold… exploded with power *(like the fireworks)*

**Narr 7:** Goodness me!

**All:** Everything's changed!

## Footnotes

There a number of songs linked to the day of Pentecost, which could be performed with various instruments. Which percussion instruments would capture the sounds of the wind, the crackling of the flames or the noise produced by many people speaking other languages? Here are some of the songs you might choose.

All over the world the Spirit is moving *(Junior Praise* 5)
Spirit of the living God *(Junior Praise* 222)
The promise of the Holy Spirit is for you *(Kidsource* 318)
Wind, wind blow on me *(Mission Praise* 771)
Jesus, send me the helper *(Kidsource* 213)
Holy Spirit, we welcome you *(Mission Praise* 241)
Glory to God, glory to God *(Peruvian Gloria)*
May your loving Spirit *(Big Blue Planet)*
I am the Church *(Big Blue Planet)*

What simple dance movements can the group develop, which will go with the words of the songs and the moods in the story?

Reproduced with permission from *Footsteps to the Feast* published by BRF 2007 (978 1 84101 464 7).

## Fancy footwork

A number of symbols and images are used to try to express the work of the invisible Holy Spirit in the lives of Christians, some of which lend themselves readily to craft activities.

**1.** Create a dove mobile using the template provided on page 227.

**2.** Using the template on page 228, cut out some flames and colour them orange, yellow and red. Collect them together to make a series of pictures that express the Holy Spirit's work in creation, Jesus and each one of us. The first picture represents a roaring fire (such as the one seen by Moses at the burning bush, which was a sign of the presence of God). The second picture is of flames arranged in a cross shape to remind us that Jesus was full of the Holy Spirit. The final picture is of flames in the shape of a person, to show that Christians are people who are filled with the Holy Spirit.

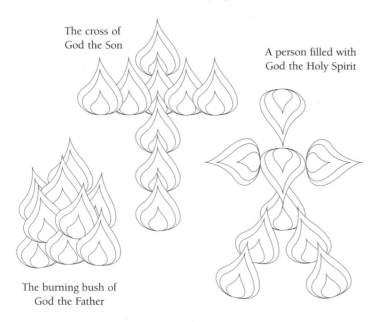

The cross of
God the Son

A person filled with
God the Holy Spirit

The burning bush of
God the Father

**3.** On large dove shapes (see the template on page 227), write different words for the fruit of the Spirit within the outline. The fruit of the Spirit can be found in Galatians 5:22–23. They are love, happiness, peace, patience, kindness, goodness, faithfulness, gentleness and self-control. Talk about these different fruits with the children as they colour them in.

## Foothold

This is a moment for worship and reflection towards the end of the programme. Draw the children together from their activities using the chant (see page 97) and have them settle down in small circles with their leaders. For each circle there should be a set of three symbols of the Holy Spirit: a flame, a dove and an open speech bubble. When the children are quiet, ask them to pass each of these symbols in turn around the circle slowly, while the leader quietly says the words below to go with each symbol.

1. **Flames:** Thank you for Pentecost and the promise of the Holy Spirit, who came like a flame to set people alight for you. Help us to burn brightly with your love in this world.
2. **Doves:** Thank you for Pentecost and the promise of the Holy Spirit, who came like a dove carried by the wind. Help us to be filled with all the special gifts we need so that we might become the best we can be for you.
3. **Open speech bubbles:** Thank you for Pentecost and the promise of the Holy Spirit, who came with words of praise in many languages. Please give us the right words to speak so that we can help each other by what we say. Thank you for the gift of the Holy Spirit at Pentecost, who changes us from 'can't do' to 'can do' people, through your strength and inspiration.

## Footsteps to the feast

Gather all the children together in one group at the centre of your space and have them sit on the floor. Before Pentecost, the disciples were a loose bunch of different people connected only by their memories of Jesus. After Pentecost, they became united people filled with and empowered by the Holy Spirit. To illustrate this whole story, direct the children's movements following each of the one-word cues as outlined below.

**Flames:** Everyone stand up where they are.

**Wind:** Everyone slowly move outwards towards the edges of the room.

**Praise:** Everyone now link hands in a great circle.

**Pentecost:** Everyone lift up their hands high, as the overall leader or a group that has practised the following words says:

*When we are weak, the Spirit makes us strong.*
*When we are afraid, the Spirit makes us brave.*
*When we feel alone, the Spirit brings God close.*
*When we feel we can't, the Spirit says, 'You can.' Amen*

## Stepping out

Finish the programme by sharing in a birthday cake together. You could choose candles for the cake that relight themselves, as a final symbol of the Spirit that keeps burning whatever happens. Invite friends and families to join you at this point as they come to collect their children.

# 7

# 3–2–1 Go!

## A special event for the feast of Trinity

The feast of Trinity comes on the Sunday immediately after Pentecost and celebrates the mystery of God as three persons in one. Christians describe the fullness of God using the formula 'God the Father, God the Son and God the Holy Spirit'. This understanding of God is drawn from the teachings of the Bible and the life and words of Jesus in particular.

It is not an easy concept for adults, let alone children, to understand, and for many outside the Christian faith it can seem as if Christians are worshipping not one God but three. This is a particular stumbling block to Jews and Muslims, who firmly believe that there is only one God. In fact, Christians believe this too, but they see God in action in three distinct ways: as the creator, the redeemer and the sanctifier. They believe that the hidden face of God the Father was made visible on earth as Jesus, and that the life of God the Son is experienced in Christians as the Holy Spirit, who is the invisible God living inside people.

The Trinity is the Church's attempt to embrace the experience of these three elements of the Godhead, and celebrates this fuller understanding of the true character of God. The feast of Trinity reminds each of us that we owe our existence, our salvation and the possibility of new life and change to this reality. What follows is a two-hour programme to present this truth in some lively and memorable ways using story, games, craft and drama.

## Bible footsteps

The material for this programme is taken from the story of the baptism of Jesus. The story can be found in all four Gospels (Matthew 3; Mark 1:4–11; Luke 3:1–22; John 1:19–34) and contains within it a clue to the Trinity.

# First steps

Welcome the children to their special day of games, stories, drama and craft. Introduce the theme of 'one into three and three into one' with some simple number-related warm-up exercises, such as the following.

**1.** Get ready for a sprint race, using different poses for 'on your marks', 'get set' and 'go' as your 3–2–1 action positions.

**2.** Pretend to travel by three different sorts of cycle: on a child's tricycle (with knees up as high as possible as you squash yourself on); on a bicycle (with head down and hands gripping the handle-bars as if riding a racer); on a unicycle (hands out wide for balance and turning suddenly left and right on the spot).

**3.** Do some finger exercises, counting 1, 2 and 3 as you put up one finger after another and then down again, counting in reverse. Now do it with both hands at the same time; try going faster and faster.

**4.** Get everyone doing other workout exercises which involve three different actions put together, such as:

- ❂ Stretching, bending and jumping
- ❂ Touching heads, then shoulders, then knees
- ❂ Putting both feet together and, jumping up and down three times only, turning a complete circle

It may also be helpful to have a joining activity as the children arrive and register. For example, play a treasure hunt game around your meeting area, in which children in threes have to find three matching objects that you have hidden. These could be real items or pictures on cards. You could include three paper plates, three plastic spoons, three paper cups, three pieces of ribbon in the same colour, and three post-it notes of the same design and colour. All the items can then be slipped into or over each other to give the impression that they are not three but one.

## Footsteps chant

Teach the following rhythmical chant as a way to move children between activities and also as a signal to draw them together to listen to instructions or to the story. Clap and call out this simple poem.

> *1, 2, 3—discover a mystery*
> *3, 2, 1—of the Father, Spirit, Son.*
> *1, 2, 3—is all of God for me.*
> *3, 2, 1—our God is three in one.*

## First footing

Introduce your fellow team members and then choose one in particular who is a father. Interview this male leader briefly to draw out more about him and, in particular, the fact that he is someone's son (where do his parents live?), that he is someone's father (are his children here today?), and that he is someone's friend (where do they usually meet up?). So, how can we describe this leader?

Prepare three large labels with the following wording in italics highlighted. (Change the leader's name, of course, to match the person you have chosen.)

To his children, he is *James the father*.
To his parents, he is *James the son*.
To his mates, he is *James the friend*.

Does this mean that James is three people? Link the fact that he is just one person to the fact that there is so much to know about God that we can only ever understand a small amount. Christians focus on three different sides of God in particular and this is how they describe him: as God the Father, God the Son and God the Holy Spirit (who, in an invisible way, can be close to everyone, everywhere, as a best friend).

When Christians want to pray for each other, they often use these three ways of describing God. They speak or bless people in the name of 'God the Father, God the Son and God the Holy Spirit'. These may be three names, but there is only one God.

Teach some simple actions to go with these three different ways of describing God. For example:

☺ **God the Father who made the world**: describe a circle with both hands.
☺ **God the Son, who rescued the world**: make the sign of the cross with one hand.
☺ **God the Spirit, who gives power to the people of God**: link your hands by the thumbs and place them splayed over your heart. Then give a series of short jumps. The hands linked by the thumbs mean that you could easily turn this into an action for a bird, like a dove. This is another helpful way of describing the Holy Spirit and comes up in the story later.

## Footbridge

Here is a selection of games that you could play on the theme of Trinity, either with all the children or in groups:

## Three-in-one clothes

Divide the group into three teams. Provide each team with the same set of three items of clothing: a soft hat, a jacket and a scarf. At a given signal, one member of the team each time must put on these three items of clothing as quickly as possible. However, with each new turn, each person in the team must wear the items in a different way. How many ways can each team think up of wearing the three items as one set of clothes?

## Three-in-one challenge

Pass around various items among your group. As individuals or teams, the children should try to come up with three different ways in which the same object could be used. Encourage them to use their imagination as vividly as possible. Objects could include a cardboard tube, a piece of hose, a plain piece of cloth, a coloured square of plastic, a twig from a shrub, a juggling ball, a ball of cotton wool, a jam jar, a piece of bamboo cane, a CD and so on.

## Three-in-one statues

In teams of three, challenge the group to create self-supporting statues with the following definitions:

- ✪ The statue should be all joined up, but there should only be three feet on the ground (and no other support).
- ✪ The statue should be all joined up, but there should only be three hands on the ground (and no other support).
- ✪ The statue should be all joined up, but there should only be one foot, one hand and one bottom touching the ground (and no other support).

## Three illustrates one

In teams of three, play a game of group charades, in which three people have to mime the following phrases or words, which are all linked to three in some way. Can the others guess what they are miming? Include blind mice, French hens, musketeers, a hat-trick, wishes, guesses, little pigs, Goldilocks' bears and so on.

## Three-in-one hunt

Play a game of linking up three words with a fourth word that connects them all. Write these words out on pieces of card first and hide them around the room. In teams, the children should try to collect as many complete sets as possible. Here are the sets:

- ✪ Composer, musician, instrument = music
- ✪ Sap, branch, leaves = tree
- ✪ Filament, bulb, electricity = light
- ✪ Hub, spokes, tyre = bicycle wheel
- ✪ Body, mind, spirit = human being
- ✪ Egg, caterpillar, cocoon = butterfly
- ✪ Writing paper, envelope, stamp = letter
- ✪ Page, cover, binding = book
- ✪ Hand, pen, ink = writing
- ✪ Faith, hope, love = virtues

## Best foot forward

Here is a way of telling the story of the baptism of Jesus with all the children together, inviting them to get involved in some simple drama. For props, you will need a blue sheet, something camel-coloured for John to wear and a simple drape for Jesus. Gather the children in a circle, but with a good clear space in the middle where the action will take place.

Introduce the story by laying across the circle the blue sheet folded into a long, thin strip. Begin the story with the words 'Something strange was happening down by the river. Someone was shouting at the top of his voice.'

Invite someone to play the part of John. This person needs to have a good shouting voice! Teach them this line: 'Change your ways! Get ready for the Lord!'

Practise this several times loudly and, as each new piece of the drama is added, return to the character of John to hear this message shouted again.

Continue with the story by saying, 'All sorts of people heard that something strange was going on down by the river and so they all came to see for themselves.'

You will now need five groups of people (of whatever numbers you can manage, according to the total size of your group). Introduce each of these groups, one at a time, and make sure they each establish their actions and words before the next group is introduced. Don't forget, in between each group, to return to John to hear him shouting his message for everyone. If possible, assign an adult leader to each group to prompt their words and movements.

- **Group 1: the soldiers:** This group should march around the circle using the chant 'Left, right; left, right; do what we tell you.'
- **Group 2: the tax collectors:** This group should creep around the circle using the chant 'Money from him, money from her; all the more for me.'
- **Group 3: ordinary people:** This group should walk around the circle shaking their heads selfishly with the chant 'This is mine and not for you; I'll keep it for myself.'
- **Group 4: the Pharisees:** This group should walk tall and proudly around the circle to the chant of 'We're God's chosen; so listen to us.'
- **Group 5: the king and his court:** This group should stay in one place and keep their distance from John with the chant 'I'll do what I like, so go take a hike!'

As the story unfolds, introduce the arrival of each group punctuated by the shouting from John. Build this up so that it becomes a real chorus of chants and shouting. Something very strange was going on by the river!

Say, 'John demanded that each group should change their ways.' Ask the children how they think each of the groups could change their ways. What might John have said to them? Perhaps it might have been something like 'Don't bully others', 'Don't be greedy', 'Don't be selfish' and so on. Ask the children to suggest what other things John might have said.

Some of the people did change their ways. To show this, take one or two from each of the groups up to John in turn. They should bow down and be covered by the blue sheet for a short moment—being 'baptized' as a sign that they want to change and be different. John could say the words 'Be baptized and get ready for the Lord.' Some from each of the groups should be 'baptized', but the group around the king do not get involved. You might mention that the king (King Herod) was so angry with what John was saying about him that eventually he arrested John and put him into prison.

While these baptisms were going on, something else very strange happened. John's cousin Jesus appeared (choose someone to play the part of Jesus). Jesus went right up to John, who was standing in the water, and asked John to baptize him. John was shocked because he recognized that Jesus was the 'Lord' he was talking about. John told Jesus that he, John, should be the one to be baptized by Jesus. But Jesus said that, for now, it should be the other way around.

Invite the child chosen to play the part of Jesus to bend down and be covered by the blue sheet of water as he is 'baptized'. Describe to the children what was heard and seen when this happened. There was a voice from heaven ('This is my own dear Son and I am pleased with him') and the Spirit of God in the form of a dove alighted upon Jesus. You could emphasize this with some appropriate actions for the dove and by cupping your hands around your mouth to make a 'microphone' for God's words. The three sides to the character of God were together in one place: Father, Son and Holy Spirit.

Jesus was very special. The people nearby saw his baptism and began to follow Jesus rather than John. John had done his work. At the conclusion of the story, ask the following questions:

☉ I wonder how John felt as he baptized his cousin, Jesus?
☉ I wonder what the crowds made of the voice and the dove?
☉ I wonder what John was thinking as he saw people start to follow Jesus and not him?
☉ I wonder if the crowds understood that God was in the voice, in the dove and in Jesus?

## Footrest

Make time for a drink and a biscuit for the children before the next stage of the journey.

## Footprints

Arrange the next set of activities so that each group has an opportunity to experience a session working on drama activities ('Footlights'), a music and dance activity ('Footnotes') and craft ('Fancy footwork').

### Footlights

Begin this drama workshop with a simple warm-up exercise. You could continue the Trinity theme in this way.

1. Teams of three should work out some synchronized movements that the group will do together (moving as one) to go from one

side of a room to the other. They must move as a single unit and try to include as many different types of movement as possible.

**2.** Continuing in threes, ask each group to become the three parts of an integrated machine that is producing one single product. Help them to decide on a product (for example, a packet of crisps, a football, an ice cream, a newspaper and so on). They should each keep their product a secret. Now the groups can work on the connected actions that they will perform as a machine to produce these items. Can the other groups guess what 'one thing from three' is being produced?

**3.** Now give out a short synopsis of one or two of the following Bible stories, all of which involve threes in some way. Set the group or groups the challenge of trying to act out the story in under one minute, with or without words. Here are the stories, which in their own way are also clues to the Trinity:

⚙ The three visitors to Abraham (Genesis 18:1–15)
⚙ Daniel's three friends in the furnace (Daniel 3:1–30)
⚙ Peter, James and John go up the mountain with Jesus (Matthew 17:1–8)
⚙ Three gifts brought by wise men to Jesus (Matthew 2:1–12)

I wonder what clues to the Trinity each story gives.

## Footnotes

Another useful analogy of the three-in-one of the Trinity has a musical connection. Every piece of music that you hear is made up of three parts: there is the composer who created it in the first place, the instrument(s) that produce the (invisible) sounds, and the performer who plays the notes. In a similar way, God the creator is the great composer, Jesus is the human performer we see who played God's tune perfectly for us to hear, and the music itself is the Holy Spirit who mysteriously touches and inspires us beyond words.

Some simple songs about the Trinity include:

Father, we adore you (*Mission Praise* 139)
Father, we love you (*Mission Praise* 142)
There is a redeemer (*Mission Praise* 673)

Two of these songs can be sung as rounds, and this is another way of musically illustrating the Trinity, as different tunes blend together as one. Once the group becomes familiar with the words and tune, they might also like to work on some movements to the music that would illustrate 'three working together as one'.

With younger children, you might prefer to stick with counting songs, such as 'One, two, three, Jesus loves me' (*Junior Praise* 189). Or you might use familiar tune 'London's burning, London's burning' but with these new words for Trinity:

> *God the Father, God the Father*
> *Made the world, made the world.*
> *Sing praise, sing praise,*
> *Let us thank him, let us thank him.*

> *God the Son, God the Son*
> *Died to save us, died to save us.*
> *Sing to Jesus, sing to Jesus,*
> *He won't leave us, he won't leave us.*

> *God the Spirit, God the Spirit*
> *Comes to help us, comes to help us.*
> *Sing praise, sing praise,*
> *He is with us, he is with us.*

If you think you and the group are up for it, you might like to tackle a song that has three (or more) parts, such as some of the music from the Wild Goose Community on Iona—for example, 'Amen, alleluia' and 'Ameni', both of which can be found in *There Is One among Us* by John Bell. You might also try 'Halle, Halle, Halle' or 'Amen Siakudumisa', both of which can be found in *Many and Great*.

## Fancy footwork

Here are some craft suggestions to help the children explore this festival theme. There is also an outline for a Trinity mosaic in *Celebrations Make & Do* published by *Barnabas* (see page 233 for details).

### Three-in-one pictures

Using only the number three (3) and the number one (1), create a drawing that contains as many objects or people as possible. Perhaps the children could do this in teams with large sheets of paper. For example, two threes together and a one could become a tree, a three on its side might be a bird in the sky, and so on.

### Dovetailing doves

Cut out five dove shapes using the template provided on page 227. This design is similar to the one used by the Catholic Church for its millennium logo. The five doves can be linked up via the head and beak to become a wheel-like circle. They can also be arranged to create a cross, with two doves becoming the arms and three making the upright. In this way, the same shape can be used to create symbols that point to God as creator (the circle of the world), God as redeemer (the cross) and God as the Spirit (place all the doves one on top of the other to make one dove outline).

One side of each dove could be coloured in greens and blues to make the world shape, and the other side in reds, oranges and yellows for the cross outline and, individually, as a reminder of the flame, which is another symbol of the Holy Spirit.

## Triangles, triangles everywhere

This activity needs more preparation, but could be used as a way into talking about the Trinity using the symbol of a triangle. You will need to prepare nine equilateral triangles to create one set with which to work. If you make them large enough, one set could be used by a group of children. Once you have the nine triangles, divide them into two piles of five and four. The triangles in the pile of five should be marked by putting a blue dot at the top, a red dot in the bottom left angle, and a yellow dot in the bottom right angle. Those in the pile of four should be marked by putting a blue dot at the top, a yellow dot in the bottom left angle, and a red dot in the bottom right angle.

The challenge now is to link up all nine triangles as one big triangle (three by three). Wherever the triangles meet, there should be three primary colours together (blue, red and yellow) and, at the centre where six triangles meet, there should be two blue, two red and two yellow dots all together.

● God the Father
● God the Son
● God the Holy Spirit

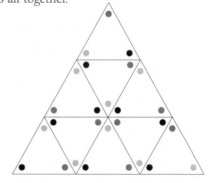

These primary colours could represent the Trinity from whom all colours come: blue for the Father, red for the Son and yellow for the Holy Spirit. Once you have created your large shape, you could put the words 'God the Father' in the top triangle, 'God the Son' in the bottom left triangle and 'God the Holy Spirit' in the bottom right triangle. The other six triangles could be filled with ways in which the Trinity is experienced by Christians today, with words such as 'God makes', 'God loves', 'God rescues', 'God forgives', 'God fills', 'God changes' and so on.

Finally, if each of the triangles is now linked to its neighbouring triangles with a small piece of clear tape, it should be possible to fold them all together to show one single triangle, and this could be kept as a visual aid of the Trinity.


## Foothold

For this reflective part of the programme, the children should be in groups on the floor, each group sitting in a triangle formation with equal sides. For example, a group of eight children and one leader would sit with one person at each of the three corners and two people between them on every side.

Today's event has been about three being one and one being three, just like the three sides making up the one triangle, in which we are sitting.

Now, into the centre of each of these triangles the leader should set out three circles of white felt, each overlapping the other to create another triangle. As the circles are put down, use these words: 'Today we have discovered that God is three but also one.'

Next, as the leader says each of the lines that follow, place a different visual on each of the three white circles as directed.

'There is God the Creator, who made us.' *(Put down a picture of a globe printed from the computer or cut from an old atlas)*

'There is God the Redeemer, who rescues us.' *(Put down a small cross)*

'There is God the Sustainer, who strengthens us.' *(Put down a picture of a flame and a dove)*

Now use the following wondering questions to prompt the children to think of what the Trinity might mean for them.

- ❂ I wonder which part of God in this picture you like the best?
- ❂ I wonder which part of God is the most important part?
- ❂ I wonder if we can leave out any part of this picture of God and still have all of God that we need?
- ❂ I wonder why Christians describe God in three parts like this?
- ❂ I wonder which part of God you feel closest to at the moment?

After a short silence, end this section with the festival chant, while the leader carefully collects up the focal items from the centre of the triangle.

## Footsteps to the feast

At the end of the event, once everything has been sorted and collected and announcements given, you could use this special circle activity to finish.

Organize the children to stand in three equal circles next to each other. Now, in their separate circles, the children should walk the circumference, keeping the shape of their circle as they make it 'turn'.

Explain that they are going to link up the three circles so that they all interlock in the same way as the three parts of God connect to become one. The circle in the centre should stay put, while the circles on either side should move into it and overlap the centre circle slightly from either side. There should be four overlapping points.

Now, as you use the festival chant, start the circles moving again, taking care that where they overlap the children don't bump into each other, but keep walking in their particular circle. The three are now becoming one!

To take this one stage further, you could also try the idea that at the points where the children cross over, those who meet should exchange the circle they are walking in, so that all the children will slowly move from circle to circle. This will need some choreography and, at its best, should look rather like formation dancing. The children are now literally moving in one circle by moving through all three—three in one and one in three. Keep this movement going to the rhythm of the chant as long as you can.

## Stepping out

If possible, end the event with some refreshments. Invite parents and carers to join in if they are not already with you, so that they can join in the celebration and see what the children have been doing. An ideal food would be cakes in the shape of triangles, or biscuits with three different ingredients.

# 8

# Bible pioneers!

## A special event to celebrate the early Church, with a focus on St Barnabas

The months of June and July include special feast days for a number of pioneer apostles and leaders of the early Church. The feast day of the apostles Peter and Paul is celebrated on 29 June. Thomas' feast day is on 3 July and James' is on 25 July. Also included in this period is a special day for Barnabas (11 June), who, as an early convert from Cyprus, played a leading role in the church in Jerusalem before accompanying Paul on his first missionary journey.

These first pioneers of Christianity often found themselves sharing the story of Jesus in countries far from home. For example, Thomas is said to have reached South India. By God's power at work in their lives, the apostles achieved things that they had never dreamed possible. Meeting Jesus had turned their lives upside down and set them on an adventure that transformed the world of their day.

However, we must not forget that these action heroes of the Church were nevertheless very ordinary people like you and me. It was the Holy Spirit who made the difference in their lives and that same Spirit is available to us today, received through faith in Christ. He promises to enable all of us, adults and children alike, to become the best we can be—pioneers for God, making a difference for good in this world.

The following outline for a special day focuses on the life of

Barnabas and has the aim of encouraging children to discover their own special work to do for God as they follow Jesus.

## Bible footsteps

The story of Barnabas' generous gift can be found in Acts 4:32–37. The story of Barnabas' encouraging welcome can be found in Acts 9:26–30. The story of Barnabas at Antioch can be found in Acts 11:19–30, and the story of when Barnabas set sail for Cyprus and beyond can be found in Acts 13.

# First steps

Welcome the children to this special Bible pioneers day. Explain that pioneers are people who are the first to do something special, whether it is attempting daring deeds or blazing some new trail. They are those who take risks and are prepared to start something new. Ask the children if they are ready to be pioneers today. If so, they will need to be fit.

Run through a simple workout activity, such as flexing muscles, stretching limbs, doing some simple knee bends, touching toes, maybe some press-ups, and exercising joints in various ways. Finally, ask the group to think of a particular favourite superhero of theirs and then, on the count of three, to freeze as that super-hero in action. Can the others identify each of these superhero statues in your hall of fame?

The story they are going to explore on this special day is about one of God's pioneers from the Bible, who shared the story of Jesus in word and deed, experiencing much opposition and many challenges. Such pioneers have a particular statue shape of their own. Demonstrate this by standing upright with your arms straight out either side in the shape of a cross. Explain that this is the important shape for a pioneer with God, as they try to live like Jesus did, caring for and bringing God's love to all.

### Footsteps chant

Here is a special chant for the day, which you could teach to a simple clapping rhythm. Use it whenever you need to bring the children together after an activity and between the sections of the day.

*We're on a special journey*
*With famous pioneers*
*Who showed God's love and changed the world*
*Throughout two thousand years.*

## First footing

Run through the following simple poem as a way of a reminding the children about the first people chosen by Jesus to follow him.

*Peter, James, Andrew, John*
*Were the first to follow on;*
*Philip, Thomas, Bartholomew*
*Began to follow Jesus too.*
*Then Judas, Jude, James, Simon,*
*With Matthew, chose to come along.*

Jesus chose these twelve disciples to be with him. At this point, ask twelve children to stand up. Explain how the disciples went everywhere with Jesus, watching how he loved and cared for people. They listened to his stories and his words about God. They began to see new things and be changed. These twelve friends told others about Jesus, too. Ask each child who is standing to choose someone else to come and stand with them. This larger group was sent out by Jesus to go and do the sort of things that he did, so that many more people were touched by God's love and were changed.

After Jesus had died on the cross and risen again on Easter morning, God sent his Holy Spirit to fill these people, so that it would be like having Jesus always with them on the inside. His followers were God's pioneers, sent to tell people of God's great love for the world and about how the bad in all of us can be beaten because of what Jesus did on the cross.

Ask those standing up to turn to others who are still sitting down and raise them up so that eventually everyone is on their feet.

These first pioneers helped many people to join God's kingdom, which we call the Church, and this kingdom has now spread right around the world. Ask the children to join hands and spread out gradually to become as large a circle as possible.

End this retelling of an outline to the story by using the day's chant (see above); then bring the children back together and sit them down again.

God has a special piece of work for each of us to do for him. Today we are exploring one story of a pioneer who did what God had planned for him to do. The pioneer's name was Barnabas and his name means 'the encourager'.

## Footbridge

Here are a few simple games that link to the idea of strengthening or encouraging each other.

**1.** Have the children stand in a large circle and give them each a number: 1, 2 or 3. Ask all those who are 'ones' to come and stand in the middle of the circle. One of the children, or maybe a young leader, should then be chosen as the 'discourager'. Moving only within the area of the circle, the children must try to avoid being touched by the discourager. If anyone is touched, he or she must sit down on the floor. The others who are still on the move can encourage the sitting ones back into the game by reaching down and briefly holding both their hands. They can then get up and start running around again.

Play to a time limit and take note, after that time, how many people are still on the move. Repeat the game but this time with all the 'twos' in the group and, finally, with the 'threes'. Which group managed to have the most people encouraged and on the move at the end of the same time limit?

**2.** Divide the group into three or four teams. Each team member in turn has to run to an appointed spot, a short distance away, and then back again. However, each team member must do it in a different style of movement, prescribed by the leader—for example, hopping on the left foot, hopping on the right foot, walking backwards, walking on all fours, skipping, walking on heels, jumping with both feet together and so on. The rest of the team should be shouting as loudly as possible to encourage the team member who is currently on the move. When someone encourages us, we are usually able to perform much better.

**3.** Play a game of four-way tug-of-war. This is another game that depends not just on teamwork but also on positive encouragement. Lay two long ropes across each other to form an equal-armed cross. Where they cross, tie them together with another thinner rope and mark the knot clearly with a colourful piece of cloth. Divide the children into four teams, equally balanced by age and strength. Each team should then pick up the rope at their end of the cross and, on a given signal, begin to pull. There should be lots of shouts of encouragement from each team. After a given time limit, all the children should stop pulling. Then the leader can take note of which team has drawn the colourful central knot closest to them.

## Best foot forward

Barnabas got the nickname 'the encourager' because of the way he helped the first pioneers of the Church. Use four areas of your hall or meeting area to tell the following story. You will need the children in four groups to help you do this. Each one should work out a particular freeze-frame (a still photo), which you will incorporate into your story. Have them practise it a few times and then, as you reach the relevant part of the story, they should stand and present their freeze-frame. Here are the four frames:

1. A group of people who have received a surprising gift from a friend.
2. One person welcoming another while everyone else looks on, suspicious and unhappy.
3. A group of people in a circle listening intently to two speaking in the middle.
4. A group of people waving goodbye to two others who are setting sail on a boat.

Now tell the story.

The early Church was growing fast. More and more people were believing in Jesus and being filled with the Holy Spirit. The believers really cared for each other, just as Jesus had said they should. They made sure that no one was in need. If one person had more food or clothes than they needed, they shared with those who hadn't enough. Outsiders were so impressed by this that they were drawn to ask questions about Jesus, and so the Church kept growing.

Joseph, who came from Cyprus, was attracted to the Church in just this way. He became a follower of the way of Jesus and, because he had more land than he needed back home in Cyprus, he sold some of it and gave the money as a gift to the Church. It was such an encouraging thing to do. The leaders were very grateful. It earned him the nickname of Joseph 'the encourager', which in Hebrew is 'Barnabas'.

Ask the first freeze-frame to stand, capturing this very scene. You could take it further and interview some of the children in the picture. What do people think about what Barnabas has just done? Why did he do it? What will they use the money for?

The first pioneer followers of Jesus did not always have an easy time. The leaders from the temple in Jerusalem tried to prevent them from talking about Jesus, but could not do so. Jesus was so important to them: even being put into prison didn't stop them. One of those who was really against the Church was a man called Saul, but something amazing happened to him on a journey. He, too, became a believer in Jesus. When he arrived in Jerusalem, the Church didn't really believe that he was a changed person. It was only Barnabas who had the courage to go out and welcome him. He encouraged others to accept Saul as a fellow Christian.

Ask the second freeze-frame to stand, capturing this moment of the story. Take it further by interviewing some of the children in the scene. What do they think has really happened to Saul? Do they believe it? Why is Barnabas willing to welcome him? How does Saul feel?

The Church kept growing, not just in Jerusalem, but in other cities too. In one place, called Antioch, even some people who didn't belong to the Jewish faith began to believe in

Jesus. The Jerusalem church sent Barnabas to investigate these new believers and he was really encouraged by what he saw. He invited Saul to join him and they stayed in Antioch, becoming pioneer leaders of this growing church, helping the new followers to live and love others just as Jesus did.

Ask the third freeze-frame to stand, capturing this moment of the story. Again, take it further by interviewing the children in the scene. What sort of things are Saul and Barnabas saying to the church? How should the church in Antioch start showing God's love? You could point out that this church did, in fact, take a collection to help those affected by a famine back in Jerusalem.

God had some more special tasks for pioneer Barnabas to do. After he and Saul had been in Antioch for a while, the church there decided that they wanted to send people to other places to tell people in those towns the story of Jesus, too. It was too important a thing to keep to themselves, so they prayed, and then they knew that God wanted Barnabas and Saul to travel out from Antioch as missionaries. Down at the coast, the believers waved goodbye to them. They knew that Barnabas would be faithful in telling the story of Jesus to others and that he would encourage them to go on in the Christian faith.

Ask the fourth freeze-frame to stand, capturing the last moment in the story. Again, interview some children in the scene. What did the church members think about saying goodbye to such important leaders? How did they know it was right to send these two away? What did they say to them? What sort of things might have been going on in Barnabas' head as he set sail to an uncertain future? What do you think God was going to do next?

## Footrest

Following this presentation of the story, take a break in groups and take time for a drink and a biscuit before moving into the next section of the day. Restart by using the special chant for the day (see above).

## Footprints

Divide the children into three groups. (It would be best to do this early in the session, when they are registered.) The grouping could be done by age, or each group could be a mixture of ages, which would allow for friends and brothers and sisters to stay together if they prefer. Each group will then visit each of the three following activities in turn, allowing about ten minutes for each one. Each activity works with the story creatively.

### Footlights

Barnabas was an encourager, not only because he gave such a generous gift to the church but also because he was quick to recognize 'the grace of God' in a situation, which he took steps to fan into flame. This was true about his attitude to Saul's conversion and the new church in Antioch. For a drama workshop on today's story, build on the theme of encouragement with the following ideas.

**1.** As a fun warm-up, practise together some ways we encourage each other: hearty handshakes, lively hugs, big smiles, in threes with hands around each other's shoulders, high-fives, enthusiastic actions in the manner of a team supporter and so on.

**2.** Now play some simple drama games. Ask the group to walk around the room displaying different moods—for example, tiredness that turns into alertness, weakness that becomes strength, disappointment that becomes pleasure, loneliness that becomes being loved and so on. In each case, it can be a word of encouragement that makes all the difference. Extend the idea by asking the children to get into small groups and enact these mood changes. Freeze each group in its low state and then ask a member of another group to come and whisper a word of encouragement in their ears, at which they unfreeze and become upbeat again.

**3.** Encouragement comes in different forms. Barnabas the encourager used a surprise gift, a generous welcome and a positive response. Ask the children to enact situations in which one of these encouragements happens. For example, they could all be working hard at school in the class when a parent arrives with a special gift (let them decide on the gift) for them all: act out the class response. They could all be muttering in a group about the arrival of a newcomer among them, when one of them has the courage to get up and welcome that person, encouraging the others to do the same: act this out as a group. Alternatively, they could be in two groups, one of which is making rather a lot of noise and upsetting the other. One from the quieter group goes over to talk to the others, encouraging them to come and make friends with the first group: act out how this goes.

**4.** Pick up on one of the scenes from the retelling of the story earlier (see 'Best foot forward'), building in further action and dialogue to illustrate what happens between Barnabas and the others each time. Maybe this could be rehearsed and presented at the end of the day.

## Footnotes

Learning a new musical instrument needs a lot of encouragement as well as hard work. As an example of the theme of the day, you could teach the children in your workshop to master the rudiments of a new instrument. Perhaps the quickest to pick up would be a percussion instrument such as the drums. You may be able to borrow a set from a local school. The leader of the group should teach some new beats and rhythms. Perhaps the group could tell the story of the day using fast and slow drumming to capture the excitement of the growing church, the surprise of Barnabas' gift, the suspicion about Saul's conversion, the steps Barnabas took to reach out to him, the emergence of the new, lively church in Antioch and so on.

In addition, some possible songs to use with this group on the theme of discovering the work God has for us to do include:

Stir me, Lord Jesus (Ian Craig, Daybreak Music)
This little light of mine
God's perfect plan (Paul Crouch and David Mudie, Daybreak Music)
God has got a plan (Nick Harding, Daybreak Music)
God's people aren't super brave superheroes (John Hardwick)

Barnabas used his gift of encouragement for God, and God has given all of us gifts that he wants us to use for him.

## Fancy footwork

Here is a selection of craft suggestions to illustrate the theme of Bible pioneers.

1. The children could make, colour and decorate special gift boxes as a reminder of Barnabas' special gift to the church. Use plenty of colourful paper, bows and ribbons to make an attractive container for a present. Barnabas gave a gift of money, of course, but what is actually remembered in his case is his gift of encouragement, which was even more valuable. The gift boxes the children make may not have money inside, but they can contain very precious gifts such as love, helpfulness and other invisible skills, which are a way of bringing God close to others.

**2.** Groups could make 'encouragement mosaics'. Cut out sets of hexagons from paper that children can paste together within a framework to create a colourful picture. On these hexagons they could write (or stick on), in different styles, words of encouragement from God, such as his promises from the Bible to us. For example:

Do not be afraid (Matthew 28:10)
I am with you (Matthew 28:20)
You are precious (Isaiah 43:4)
I have chosen you (Isaiah 44:1)
I call you friends (John 15:15)
I will never leave you (John 14:18)
I call you by name (Isaiah 43:1)
I know the plans I have for you (Jeremiah 29:11)

It was God's encouraging love, which we see in Jesus, that made Barnabas into the person he was and also helps us to become God's special pioneers.

**3.** You could create a symbol of welcome. The way Barnabas welcomed Saul was a vital turning point in the growth of the early Church. Just think how different things might have been if he hadn't bothered to shake Saul by the hand! How we react to others is a vital way to show and share the love of God. Older children may like to mould a model hand out of air-drying clay or play-dough, as a reminder of how an encouraging handshake can make such a difference. When the model is dry, it could be painted either silver or gold, to show that this gift of encouragement is worth far more than money.

## Foothold

Take some time at the end of the session to come together for a moment of reflection. In small groups, ask the children to sit in circles with a leader. Perhaps, with the children's permission, any craft items that have been finished can be put in the centre as a focus for the worship, or perhaps one of the drama groups could present what they have rehearsed. Now, in a moment of quiet, use the following words and actions to think back through the event.

**Leader:** Barnabas the encourager shared the gifts he had.

*Ask the children to hold out both hands together in front, palms upward, as if offering a gift.*

**Leader:** Barnabas the encourager welcomed the outsider.

*Ask the children to cross their arms, reaching out either side to their neighbours to shake hands with each other.*

**Leader:** Barnabas the encourager saw good things happening and made sure they got better.

*Ask the children to put one hand above their eyes as if looking out for something and to beckon with the other as if encouraging someone to keep going.*

**Leader:** Barnabas the encourager was ready to hear God's voice calling him to do new things.

*Ask the children to put one hand to their ear, listening out for God.*

**Leader:** God had a special work for Barnabas to do as one of his first pioneers in the Church. God has a special work for each one of us to do as God's pioneers today. I wonder what God wants us to become and to do for him.

> *Ask the children to put the forefinger and thumb of one hand on their chin in a wondering way.*

Allow a short pause and then end with this prayer:

> *Lord, thank you for the special gifts you have given each one of us. Help us to use them, as Barnabas did, to share your love in this world. Amen*

End with the chant of the day together.

## Footsteps to the feast

Here is a final activity that you could try, as a seal on this special day about one of God's pioneers. Ask the children to scatter round the room quickly and then, on a given signal, to stand completely still. Next, they should sit down where they are, crosslegged on the floor. One leader should move around in between the children. After a while, she or he should pause and choose one child, to whom s/he extends a hand, lifting that child up to join him/her. Now this child should choose someone else by whom to stop and reach out a hand to invite him or her to join them.

Continue until the whole group is up, linked hand to hand in a great chain of encouragement. Now try to link up the ends of the chain, even if this does mean ducking under each other's arms at some point. End with a great mass handshake in the chain, perhaps also using the chant of the day for the final time.

## Stepping out

Invite parents and carers to join you at the end of the session for a 'feast' together (drinks and cake). Allow the children time to collect crafts before they go home.

# 9

# Thanks a million!

## A special event to celebrate harvest festival

Although not strictly one of the great feasts of the Church, harvest is nevertheless a widely recognized occasion for Christians to celebrate God's goodness to us all. Even in today's prepackaged and refrigerated world of food products, there is still a residual awareness of how much we depend on the fruits of the earth for our survival as a species. Whenever crops fail because of drought, or imports are disrupted because of natural disasters or wars, we are quickly reminded that we are all dependent on successful harvests year by year. The evidence is also seen in attendances at harvest festival services in church, which are often among the largest in the year. As parents, we acknowledge how important it is to teach our children those vital words 'please' and 'thank you'. If this is true, how much more should we encourage a habit of heartfelt gratitude in relation to God our Father, who, we believe, sustains the annual cycle of growth on our amazingly fruitful earth.

Harvest is the opportunity to remind ourselves and to invite others to recognize that this is God's world, that he has given us more than enough for our need (though not for our greed) and that he loves to give us good things as a sign of the unfailing love he offers to every one of us.

## Bible footsteps

The Bible is rich in harvest imagery, which is no surprise, given how much more obvious it was for people in the past that they depended on a good harvest. God's goodness is seen in the abundance and extravagance of nature's gifts to us, and the Bible uses harvest images to describe the sort of lives we should live in response—for example, that we should be like a well-watered garden (Isaiah 58:11), a fruitful vine (John 15:1–10), an evergreen tree (Psalm 1:3) and an ever-flowing stream (Isaiah 48:18).

Harvest is an opportunity to build into your church's celebrations an open event where children can invite their friends to hear the story of God's goodness to us as we think about not only the harvest of the land but also the harvest of our lives. The event will focus on stories and passages from the Old Testament and includes a harvest story (the book of Ruth), a harvest hymn (Psalm 67) and a harvest parable (Isaiah 5:1–5).

The Bible background underpinning the celebration is Deuteronomy 26:1–11.

## First steps

The promise of a regular harvest is first given by God to Noah after the flood and is sealed by the sign of the rainbow (see Genesis 8:21–22 and 9:8–13).

The colours in the rainbow could be used as the names for the team groups into which the children should be divided, perhaps by age, when they arrive. The teams with their leaders can be decorating their base areas during the registration time, using objects and pictures that are of their particular colour. For this, you will need to collect the various coloured materials beforehand.

In addition, each team base should colour in one large semi-circular piece of card that has been cut to fit in with the other semicircles to create a huge rainbow backdrop, which can be used as a focus for the day.

Beneath the rainbow focus, create a simple harvest display of fruits, vegetables and flowers. Also include some large pictures that connect with the stories used in today's programme—a fruitful tree, a cornfield and a vineyard.

Once all the children have arrived, gather them together to begin the programme. Use the fact that they belong to different colour teams to introduce some simple warm-up activities. You could call out various actions to be attempted by different colours: for example, jumping up as high as possible, running to a wall and back, star jumps, hopping, skipping or running on the spot. Next, mix up the colours by asking them to pair up in particular combinations to touch knees, heads, elbows, fingertips and so on. Finally, have them arrange themselves into groups of seven (one of each rainbow colour) and, as a group, make a joined-up piece of sculpture according to the following descriptions:

- An arch
- A tiny ball
- A huge star shape, in which the children are linked by their feet, their elbows or their shoulders
- A circle

Introduce the harvest theme by reminding them of God's promise to Noah that he would always make sure there was an adequate harvest each year in the world. Sadly, some of us in certain parts of the world keep the excess of our harvests to ourselves, so it is not shared with those in need. This is all the more reason why God should talk about looking for another harvest, a harvest of goodness in our lives, which knows how to share and care for his world and his people. In today's programme, the children will be exploring some Bible stories on the theme of harvest to see what these stories might mean for them.

## Footsteps chant

Use the following chant to move the children through the programme between the sessions. Ask the children to join in with some rhythmic clapping and then to echo back to you as leader the following simple rhyme for the day, line-by-line.

*Let's celebrate the harvest*
*Of water, field and tree,*
*And see how God has given all*
*With love to you and me.*

## First footing

Gather the children together to tell them the story of Ruth under the title of 'A harvest surprise'. This is a story of one harvest that failed and another that was successful and led to an important marriage.

The book of Ruth is a story from the time when judges ruled in Israel. Naomi and her family emigrated to the country of Moab because of a famine. During their ten years away, her two sons married local Moabite women, but then both boys and Naomi's husband died. At this point, Naomi decides to return to her old home in Bethlehem and, of her two daughters-in-law, only Ruth agrees to go with her. They arrive in Bethlehem while the barley is being harvested. To support them both, Ruth works in the fields, where she meets and later marries a distant relative of her late husband, the wealthy landowner Boaz. Their great-grandson becomes the famous King David of Jerusalem.

What follows is a retelling of the story of the whole of the book of Ruth. Read it through a number of times so that you can, as far as possible, tell it without having to read every word. As a starting point, you might like to show a piece of corn freshly cut from the fields.

A stalk of corn… a sheaf of corn… a field of corn. Perhaps over the summer you saw corn like this, ripening for harvest in the fields. And that's good news. It means there will be bread in the shops… toast on our tables… and sandwiches in our lunch boxes. But imagine if the corn didn't grow, the fields remained empty and there were no sheaves or stalks of corn growing. In some parts of the world this happens, and it is bad news.

That's just the way it was hundreds of years ago in Bethlehem. The town was usually well known for its bread supplies—the name Bethlehem means 'house of bread—but not this year. This year the house was empty. There was a famine and things were bad.

Naomi's family decided it was so bad that the only answer was to move somewhere new, to go to another country where there was food. It's no easy decision, leaving your own home. It's harder still to decide to become a refugee—that's how bad it was for them. In the nearby country of Moab there was food but, sadly, things did not go well there for Naomi.

First her husband died. She must have thought it was a terrible mistake to have left Bethlehem, after all. Then her two sons, who had married local girls, fell ill and they died too. This was a real blow for Naomi. They'd moved to save their lives, not to lose them. Why, oh why, hadn't they stayed in Bethlehem? Poor Naomi was left with only her two daughters-in-law, Orpah and Ruth. Naomi was a broken woman. Can you imagine her sadness?

She'd been away from Bethlehem for ten long years by now, and all she had known was loss. However, back in

Bethlehem, things had got better so she decided to return —alone, of course, since why should Orpah and Ruth want to come with her? They had no reason to become foreigners in a strange land, no reason whatsoever—but even so, both daughters-in-law cared deeply for Naomi.

'I'm nothing but trouble and bitterness,' said Naomi. 'Why come with me? You won't really belong there and there's no guarantee I can find new husbands for you. No, stay here in your own country.' Orpah eventually agreed to stay, but Ruth cared so deeply for Naomi that she said, 'I'll go with you. I'll stay wherever you stay. I will follow your God and take the risk of leaving my home country because I care for you.' Ruth showed great loyalty and compassion.

In Bethlehem it was harvest time. Both Naomi and Ruth were so poor that they had to depend on picking up the leftovers in the fields. Naomi was too old to bend and gather corn, so Ruth did all the work. All the local people were amazed that a stranger and a foreigner like Ruth should be so kind. The owner of one field was called Boaz. He was so impressed by the story of Ruth's kindness that he invited her to join up with his servants in the harvesting. It was unexpected and unusual to show such a welcome to an outsider, but Boaz was a remarkable man. He was even more remarkable than Ruth realized, because when she told Naomi about it, Naomi remembered that Boaz was a distant cousin of her dead husband. They were related. Maybe, just maybe, God had his hand on all this after all.

Sure enough, Boaz's kindness continued and, on Naomi's advice, Ruth made a private visit to Boaz to ask for help for herself and Naomi. He was a kind man and was flattered by her attention. He agreed to help and even offered to marry Ruth, if she would have him, because he was already quite old himself. This way he would give the two women a new home and a new start.

First, though, Boaz had to do the right thing, and that involved a legal ceremony, just in case any other closer relative wanted to take care of the women. That was the custom in those days. But it all worked out and by the end of harvest there was a double celebration. Not only was the corn safely gathered in, but there was also a great wedding feast. It really was a surprise harvest for Ruth and for her mother-in-law.

Ruth's kindness and compassion had not gone unnoticed or unrewarded—not by Naomi, not by Boaz, and not by God. And that's not quite the end of the story, because Ruth had a little harvest of her own! Soon a son was born, and that son had a son, and that son had more sons and daughters. A whole 'field of corn' grew up from Ruth's family and one of those great-grandsons turned out to be none other than the great King David himself. And even that isn't the end of the story because one of David's distant, distant, distant great-great-great-grandchildren turned out to be the most compassionate person who ever lived. Can you guess who that was? How surprised Ruth would have been by this harvest!

## Footbridge

Here are some suggestions for games to follow on from the story, based on the harvest theme.

## Corn salad

Gather the children into a circle and go round giving each one the word seed, stalk or sheaf. Play a 'fruit salad' type of game, calling out one of these words, at which the children whose word it is should quickly cross the circle to the other side. Practice crossing the circle and then ask for some volunteers to be in the middle. This time, when you call out the word, the volunteers need to move and find a place back in the circle, stranding someone else in the middle. If you want everyone to move, call out the word 'harvest'.

## Guess what?

Play a game of charades, in which one child (or perhaps a whole team) has to mime eating a particular fruit. Can the others guess which fruit it is? Repeat the game with popular snacks, chocolates, sweets, main meals and desserts.

## Frozen meals

Play a game in which a leader calls out key words that are linked to particular actions. Begin with the children walking around randomly; then, as soon as they hear the key word, they must adopt the pose or action that they have been shown. For example:

- ❂ **Flowerpot:** all the children stand together with arms held high in a tight squeeze.
- ❂ **Cornfield:** all in a filled-in square formation.
- ❂ **Orchard:** all space out and stand with their hands in the air like the branches of a tree.
- ❂ **Vineyard:** all get on to the floor on their knees, holding out their hands wide to either side and linking up with each other.
- ❂ **Windfalls:** all curl up in small lumps on the ground.

## Maize maze

The children should stand in four rows, one row behind the other, all facing in the same direction. Ask them to hold out their arms to link up with those on either side of them, creating four lines of joined children. They should then all turn through 90 degrees and stretch out their arms again to link up with different neighbours— in effect, moving from horizontal lines to vertical lines (or rows to columns).

Practise doing this manoeuvre on the command 'turn' from the leader. Once they have mastered it, choose some people to be runners and some to be chasers. Separate them so that they are apart from each other among the linked rows, and then set them running. They can go round the ends of the lines, but not wander off: the chase must only happen between the lines of children. Every now and then, the leader calls out 'turn' and then the rows become columns, either helping or hindering the runners and chasers.

## Domino tree

This game aims to create a sort of family tree between all the children. Ask for one volunteer to stand in the middle. Now ask for someone who feels they could link up with this child by having a defined connection to him or her, such as, 'We go to the same school'. That child should come and link up with the one in the middle. Now ask for others to join on, either to the original volunteer or to the new link in the domino tree.

No one must use the same connecting reason twice. So, for example, the first pair might connect because they both like the same pop band, and the second because they both support the same football team, and so on. Children can join the tree at any point and any one person can have up to four connections by touching hands or feet. What sort of domino tree of connections can the whole group create?

# Best foot forward

Here is a way of walking through the story of Ruth with pauses and discussion points to connect the story with the children's lives today. You will need seven stations for the story: you could use the different base areas for the colour teams around the room. For each part of the story, you will also need a simple symbol to help focus your storytelling (see below).

Many elements of this harvest romance could be developed in conversation with the children. For example, there are the sad experiences of Naomi as an economic migrant, the experience of famine, the loyalty of Ruth, attitudes to foreigners and newcomers, care for those in need, the welcome shown by Boaz to the outsider, God's blessing on his people, the setting of Bethlehem and the connection to the family line of both King David and Jesus. At each station, ask some of the questions below to get the children talking about these issues and connecting the events long ago with life today.

## Scene 1: Bethlehem (Ruth 1:1–2)

**Symbol:** an empty plate. Tell the story of how Naomi and her family, experiencing famine in Bethlehem, decide to move away. Ask the questions:

- ❂ I wonder how hard it was for Naomi and her family to leave their home town?
- ❂ I wonder if this still happens for some people today?

## Scene 2: Moab (Ruth 1:3–5)

**Symbol:** a loaf of bread on a black cloth (for sadness). Tell the story of the family's time in Moab, where there was food, but then the sadness of the illness that took away Naomi's husband and two sons, leaving her alone with two daughters-in-law, Ruth and Orpah. Ask the questions:

- I wonder how Naomi and her family felt on arriving in a strange country, and what the people there said about them?
- I wonder if people have similar experiences today?
- I wonder what sort of prayer Naomi would have said to God in the time following the death of her husband and her two sons?
- I wonder if it's right to be angry with God sometimes?

## Scene 3: Bethlehem (Ruth 1:6–18)

**Symbol:** three women's headscarves. Tell the story of the return to Bethlehem and the decision by the daughters-in-law either to stay at home or go with Naomi. Ruth decides to go, even though it means becoming a refugee in a strange land. Ask the questions:

- I wonder why Ruth decided to stay with Naomi?
- I wonder how it felt for her to arrive as a stranger in a foreign land?
- I wonder how we would welcome a stranger from another country?

## Scene 4: The harvest field (Ruth 2:1–16)

**Symbol:** a bag of corn pieces (you could use crushed cornflakes). Tell the story of Ruth taking care of Naomi and gleaning with the others during harvest time. Note their comments and Boaz's kindness. Ask the questions:

- I wonder what the other people in the cornfield thought about Ruth?
- I wonder whether some people might have been angry that she was allowed to glean in the same way that they were?
- I wonder why Boaz acted differently?
- How can we show kindness to those in trouble?

## Scene 5: Boaz's home (Ruth 3:1–18)

**Symbol:** a pillow. Tell the story of how Ruth goes to talk with Boaz at night, explaining that she is a distant relative through Naomi and asking Boaz to take responsibility for her and Naomi. Ask the questions:

☉ I wonder how hard it was for Boaz to show his love for an outsider from a different country?

☉ I wonder what people today think about those who go out of their way to make friends with those who are very different from themselves?

## Scene 6: The city gate (Ruth 4:1–12)

**Symbol:** A sandal. Tell the story of Boaz's meeting with the others, giving a closer relative the chance to take on the responsibility of looking after Ruth, which he renounces by the symbolic action of taking off his sandal. Ask the questions:

☉ I wonder why the other relative was unwilling to take responsibility for looking after Ruth?

☉ Isn't it easier just not to get involved with difficult situations?

## Scene 7: The harvest wedding (Ruth 4:13–17)

**Symbol:** a box of confetti. Tell the story of Boaz and Ruth getting married at harvest time and how, through their family, we come to King David and then (much further off) to Jesus himself. Ask the questions:

☉ I wonder what sort of prayer Naomi said now to God, after Ruth and Boaz's wedding?

☉ I wonder whether God still changes situations so that something bad can become something good in the end?

## Footrest

Follow this active retelling of the story with a refreshment break, having drinks and biscuits in the colour teams.

## Footprints

At this point in the programme comes an opportunity for the children (and adults) to experience one or more of the following activity sessions on the harvest theme, using drama (Footlights), music (Footnotes) and craft (Fancy footwork).

## Footlights

1. The book of Ruth covers a range of emotions. Rehearse some of the following with your group and then invite them to interpret the story as you briefly retell it. They should try to show the depth of the emotions with their facial expressions and their whole body as the story develops. Here are some of the feelings and moods involved, in the order in which they appear:

- ☼ Fear of starvation
- ☼ Sadness at leaving home
- ☼ Grief at losing loved ones
- ☼ Uncertainty over what to do next
- ☼ Amazement (that Ruth decides to go with her mother-in-law)
- ☼ Loneliness on arriving in Bethlehem
- ☼ Nervousness about being out alone in the fields
- ☼ Curiosity (of Boaz and others) on hearing about the kindness of Ruth
- ☼ Excitement (of Naomi) on hearing about Boaz
- ☼ Relief and joy at the news of a marriage proposal
- ☼ Joy in the celebration on the wedding day

Invite the group to step into the whole story in this way and provide an emotional accompaniment to your storytelling.

**2.** How do we spot people in genuine need? How can we recognize how they really feel and, as a result, be able to offer genuine help? Naomi had once been an outsider in Moab, so maybe that was why she could understand how Ruth felt on arriving in Bethlehem. For Boaz, it was harder. He had to try to step into the shoes of this outsider, alone in a foreign field, to be able to respond to her with compassion.

In groups, ask the children to develop a short role-play that explores what it must feel like to be:

- ☼ The one who is left out when it comes to picking teams.
- ☼ The one who has a disability while the rest of the class are all able-bodied.
- ☼ The one who is often away ill through no fault of their own.
- ☼ The one who can't afford to wear all the latest fashionable clothes.
- ☼ The one who always seems to get things wrong and be in the way.

**3.** Who are the real outsiders today? Why do we find it so hard to relate to them? Here are some more thoughts to help apply the story to the children's world. Ask the groups to set up either freeze-frames or short dramas involving the sort of outsiders that they might come across, such as:

- ☼ The child who turns up new to your class halfway through the school year.
- ☼ A new neighbour in your street.
- ☼ Someone visiting your area or school for the day.
- ☼ A refugee from another country who is housed in your town.
- ☼ An asylum seeker whom you meet through your church or club.
- ☼ A child you meet who wears different clothes and speaks in a different way from what you're used to.

Each time, the group should show first a negative way of handling the situation and then a positive approach.

## Footnotes

There is no shortage of well-known traditional hymns for harvest, as well as plenty of general 'thank you' songs for a music workshop. Here are just some that you might consider:

Thank you Lord that this fine day (try substituting harvest food items in the verses) (*Junior Praise* 232)
We plough the fields and scatter (*Junior Praise* 267)
Who put the colours in the rainbow? (*Junior Praise* 288)
Someone's brought a loaf of bread (*Junior Praise* 220)
If I were a butterfly (*Junior Praise* 94)
God who made the earth (*Junior Praise* 63)
The fruity song (a fun play on fruit words by Jim Bailey)

You could try using some objects from the natural world to accompany the playing of one of these songs. For example:

- The two halves of a coconut shell.
- Dried peas inside a large seedpod to make a shaker.
- A piece of grass split down the middle, to make a whistling sound.
- Twigs rubbed against a piece of bark.
- A simple two- or three-hole recorder made from a piece of hollow bamboo.
- Some homemade wind chimes.

One way to begin this workshop would be to remind the children of the many natural sounds that God has given us in his world. Collect a range of such sounds. Many are recorded on sound effects CDs, which can be borrowed from the local library: for example, wind noises, bird song, sea sounds and animal calls, including the singing of whales, cicadas and dolphins. Play these sounds and see if the children can guess which gift of God's creation is making the music. Alternatively, hand out some large seashells in which you may be able to detect the sounds of the sea.

## Fancy footwork

**1.** Pick up on the theme of the rainbow in the story of Noah (Genesis 9:12–17), which reminds us of the promise of a yearly harvest. Make rainbow bracelets by plaiting together a selection of threads in rainbow colours.

**2.** Decorate some pieces of card using blow paints. Cut two parallel slits in the card, 3cm apart, about two-thirds of the way down. Now take some dried grasses or stems of wheat and thread them in between the slits, fixing them with glue. Mount this card on a slightly larger, darker background to create the effect of a picture frame.

**3.** Make a picture using variously coloured and shaped pieces of pasta, together with dried haricot beans, lentils, green split peas and sunflower seeds. This picture could be abstract or could illustrate one moment from the story of Ruth's 'harvest surprise'.

**NB:** Be careful to warn the children that raw beans are not edible, and note that small peas could be a choking hazard.

For a further idea for a harvest banner, see *Celebrations Make & Do* published by *Barnabas* (see page 233 for details).

# Foothold

Use the footsteps chant on page 144 to bring the children together for a final 'thank you' reflection. Have the children sitting in circles in their colour groups or teams, with a leader for each group. In the middle of each circle place a small globe. The following leader's words should be said centrally, while the children respond from within their circles to the visuals and the actions. This short reflection ends with a version of Psalm 67: a harvest psalm.

**Leader:** Look, look, God has given us the whole world and everything in it.

**Everyone:** Thank you, God.

**Leader:** Look, look, God has given us fruits and flowers and foods of all sorts to enjoy.

*The group leaders should place some grapes, a flower and another item of food in the middle of their circle.*

**Everyone:** Thank you, God.

**Leader:** Look, look, God has given us Jesus, born into the family whose ancestors were Ruth and Boaz and great King David.

*The group leaders should place a cross in the middle of their circle alongside the other items.*

**Everyone:** Thank you, God.

**Leader:** Look, look, God has given us days and months and years to live for him and to bring his love to others.

*The group leaders should flick through a calendar and then place it in the middle with the other items.*

Reproduced with permission from *Footsteps to the Feast* published by BRF 2007 (978 1 84101 464 7).

**Everyone:** Thank you, God.

**Leader:** Look, look, God has made you and me…

*Everyone in the group should place in the circle something that represents themselves (they will need to be forewarned about this)—maybe their name badge or a small personal possession.*

**Leader:** … and God wants our lives to be a harvest of good things, too.

**Everyone:** Thank you, God.

*A short pause.*

**Leader:** May God be kind to us and bless us.

*Each child in each team or group should hold hands.*

**Leader:** May the light of God's face shine on each one of us, so that his ways and his praise will be seen on earth. Let everyone say thank you to God.

*The overall leader calls out each of the colour groups' names and they respond with a loud shout of 'Thank you'.*

**Leader:** God has given us a good harvest. God has blessed us. Let the whole world say 'thank you'.

*Each group leader lifts their globe high.*

**Everyone:** Thank you!

Reproduced with permission from *Footsteps to the Feast* published by BRF 2007 (978 1 84101 464 7).

## Footsteps to the feast

Using the chant again, gather the children into one large circle. Each child should link up to his or her neighbour using their elbows, leaving both hands free. Now turn this circle into a 'world of thanks for harvest' as everyone begins clapping hands and the circle turns round in a great wheel of praise.

## Stepping out

Finish the programme by inviting parents and carers to join you in a real harvest feast, including some of the fruit and food that you have talked about and, of course, some items made from wheat or corn.

**NB:** Make sure you are aware of any food allergies, especially wheat allergies.

# 10

# Light refreshment!

## A special event for Hallowe'en and the feast of All Saints

If saints are 'people through whom God's light shines', then All Saints' Day should be a festival guaranteed to light up the dark. Perversely, however, it is the darkness of All Saints' Eve (Hallowe'en) that tends to steal the limelight at this time of year—just when, as Christians, we want to put God's special people into the spotlight. Many churches are concerned about this increasing emphasis on celebrating the darkness of 31 October and host alternative Hallowe'en parties to celebrate the light instead.

The following outline for such a celebration plays with the theme of God's light that beats the darkness. This is a theme found throughout the Bible story and is summed up neatly in the opening verses of John's Gospel, where John writes, 'The light keeps shining in the dark, and darkness has never put it out' (John 1:5).

As an Old Testament focus for the theme, this programme uses the story of God's appearance to Moses in the unquenchable light of the burning bush on Mount Sinai. This experience inspires Moses to take God's rescuing light to the people of God in one of their darkest hours, as slaves in Egypt. It is the light brought by Moses that brings the people of God out of that darkness into the light of freedom; it is a light that continues to guide and challenge them on their desert journey.

This feast is an opportunity to celebrate the light that God promises to all of us because of the light of Christ, who has beaten death and darkness for ever through the cross. As John again writes, this time in his first letter, 'God is light and doesn't have any darkness in him... if we live in the light, as God does, we share in life with each other. And the blood of his Son Jesus washes all our sins away' (1 John 1:5, 7).

## Bible footsteps

The story can be found in Exodus 3:1–10. References are also made to the whole Exodus story, found in chapters 4—15.

# First steps

Introduce the theme of lighting up the dark with a treasure hunt game as the children arrive. Hide light-related items (or pictures of them) around the hall or meeting area before the children arrive: for example, a torch, a candle, a light bulb, a matchbox, some fairy lights, a lantern, a bicycle light; a picture of a lighthouse, the sun, stars and moon, traffic lights, a bonfire or street lights. Give the children, or teams of children, pencil and paper. They then have to find all the light-related items or pictures. As they find each item, they write its name on their piece of paper. Tell them how many items are hidden in total, so that they know when they have completed the search.

Also at registration time, divide your group into teams and allocate team areas and team leaders. The names of the teams could be linked to some of the treasure hunt light images that you have used, such as the Spotlights, the Candle Flames, the Shooting Stars, the Torch Beams and so on. The team bases can also be decorated in ways appropriate to their names, using bright yellows or whites against dark backgrounds, along with examples of different types of light source.

Once all the children have arrived, gather them centrally to welcome them and introduce them to the programme. Start with some fun warm-up exercises based around activities that link to the lights they have been searching for in the treasure hunt. For example:

Candles: hands together as if in prayer above their heads and 'flickering'.

Lighthouses: arms out in front, with hands together like a beam of light, then revolving on the spot.

Stars: hands up high, then rapid opening and closing of the fingers to imitate the twinkling of the stars.

Traffic lights: when the leader calls out 'green', everyone runs around the room. When the leader calls 'amber', everyone continues running, but in slow motion. Finally, when the leader calls 'red', everyone freezes.

Fairy lights: all do star jumps on the spot.

Spotlights: everyone stand frozen in a dramatic pose, as if on stage.

Sunlight: everyone curl up as a ball.

Moonlight: all stand curved like a crescent moon.

Headlights: everyone walk around with their arms out in front, wide apart for full headlights, then with hands dipped down towards the left for dipped lights. In the process of moving around, no one should crash into anyone else!

Matches: everyone stand still and become as tall as possible, on tiptoes and reaching high. When the leader says 'strike a light', everyone should make some flickering movements of their body and slowly shrivel up, smaller and smaller.

After this, have the children sit down so that you can unpack the day's theme. Explain that you are all going to discover how God's light is stronger than all darkness. God shines his light through his people, who then take it out into the dark places of the world. God's saints are those who are filled with his light and who also know that God's light burned brightest and best in the life of Jesus, who called himself 'the light for the world'. God wants each one of us to be a light for him, to help rescue all the people in this world who are trapped in the dark.

## Footsteps chant

Teach a theme chant for the event, which you can use in between the various activities. Start by creating a simple clapping rhythm and then ask everyone to repeat each line of the following short poem, after you as leader. Do this several times, varying pace, pitch and volume.

*We are on a special journey*
*Of stories from the Book.*
*To see the light that beats the dark,*
*It's here we're going to look.*

## First footing

Introduce the story of Moses and the light that will not go out by lighting a relightable candle. Every time you blow the candle out, it will relight. (Take care when handling the candle and have some water ready to extinguish it completely when you have finished the demonstration.) Tell the story using mime actions alongside each piece of narration. Encourage the children to imitate these actions in order to help them step into the story.

Say that this story is about a bright light that just would not go out, and because of that, it got noticed.

Once, a shepherd called Moses was leading his sheep up among the wild, rocky foothills of Mount Sinai. He was on the lookout for some good green grass to feed his flock.

*Action: walking on the spot looking to the left and right, shading your eyes with one hand.*

Moses was far from home. He was tired and the day was getting hot.

*Action: yawning and sighing; wipe the sweat from your brow, saying 'phew'.*

Suddenly Moses saw something strange. It was a very bright light that wasn't the sun. It was something up on the slope near by.

*Action: stop still and point to one side, looking puzzled.*

It was a bush on fire—a real blaze! However, the strange thing was that the flames didn't die away as you would normally expect to happen with such fires. They kept burning brightly.

*Action: Moses scratches his head, knits his brows and makes a puzzled gesture.*

Moses decided to take a closer look.

*Action: pretend to walk up a slope, slowly and carefully.*

As Moses came near to the bush, he could feel the heat of the flames, and its bright light dazzled his eyes.

*Action: shield your face from the heat and light.*

Suddenly Moses heard a voice calling his name: 'Moses. Moses.' The bush was talking to him!

*Action: Moses opens his mouth in amazement.*

Moses looked around to check that no one was watching. After all, it isn't every day you start talking to a bush! Then he said, 'Yes, it's me. Here I am.'

*Action: all repeat Moses' words.*

Then the voice said, 'I am the Lord God.' Moses gasped.

*Action: everyone gasps.*

Then Moses buried his head in his hands and knelt down.

*Action: follow these movements.*

'Take off your shoes,' said the Lord. 'This is a really special place.' Moses did as he was told.

*Action: mime taking off shoes and then stepping forward slowly.*

The bush was full of a light that kept on burning very bright. This light looked as if it could last for ever. God said, 'I am God—the God who spoke to your ancestors, to Abraham, Isaac and Jacob.' Moses was now very afraid and hid his face in his hands.

*Action: follow this movement.*

After all, he knew that no one could see God and live to tell the tale!

Then God gave this message to Moses. 'Listen, Moses. I know how dark things have got for my people in Egypt. I've seen how much they are suffering and in how much danger they are. I'm coming to rescue them. I will bring them light in their darkness. I will be the light that leads them to a new, safe place, where they can live in light and freedom.' Moses listened carefully and was amazed. 'Wow!'

*Action: everyone repeats, 'Wow!'*

Then God said, 'And I'm going to send you to do this for me. I want you to be the one who brings my rescuing light to my people.' Moses was very shocked. He said, 'Who, me?'

*Action: everyone repeats Moses' words.*

'No way,' said Moses. 'This is way out of my league. I can't do this.'

*Action: everyone shakes their head vigorously.*

Moses began to make up excuse after excuse, but God had spoken. God knew that Moses was the right man for the job. God's light was going to shine through him to light up the darkness and rescue his people.

I wonder how you would feel if God had given you a message like that?

I wonder what excuses you would have made to avoid such a scary mission?

*Link this to the excuses that Moses did make, such as, 'I'm not a good speaker'; 'They won't believe me'; How will they know it is really God who has sent me? (See Exodus 3:11–13; 4:1, 10.)*

I wonder if God's saints down the ages felt like Moses when God called them to do something special? I wonder if they often didn't feel up to the job?

God's light can change people as well as situations. It shines into our lives so that we can end up doing things we never imagined possible.

## Footbridge

Here are some light-related games that you could play with the group.

**1.** Darken the room as much as possible and then challenge one representative from each team to spell out a simple word with the light of a torch, so that the others in his or her team can guess what is being spelled.

**2.** Play a version of tag. One person is 'it' and has a torch. If he or she can keep the torch beam on another player for a leader's count of five, that player is captured and becomes 'it' instead. Everyone should be encouraged to dodge and duck as much as possible, to avoid being held in the torch beam.

**3.** Cut out lots of star shapes from newspaper sheets and attach them to the floor of the room. Have one star for every child. Play some appropriate music. When the music stops, everyone should stand on a star. Now continue the game, but each time remove one of the stars. The child who does not make it on to a star when the music stops becomes part of a panel of judges to see fair play as the game proceeds. Keep removing a star so that there is always one fewer than the number of children playing at any one time.

**4.** Play a game in teams in which each team member in turn has to run to a fixed point to collect the components for a torch. Dismantle some torches into as many parts as possible, including the bulb, the handle, two batteries, a bulb cover, as well as the box into which the torch goes and a bag into which to put the box.

Each child runs to collect one of the items, but must do so in a particular style based on the team's name. For example, those in the Lighthouse team should run with arms held out in front while turning circles at the same time; those in the Shooting Stars team run doing regular star jumps; those in the Spotlight team keep their feet together and move only by jumping; those in the Candlelight team move along on their knees with their hands above their heads, and so on. The first team to collect and assemble their torches, then to stand grouped together with their torch lighting up their faces, is the winner.

## Best foot forward

In this section, tell the story of how Moses went on to lead the people out of the darkness of slavery into the light of freedom by crossing the Red Sea (also known as the Reed Sea, or the Sea of Reeds). This idea is based on an original piece by Lucy Moore of the *Barnabas* ministry team.

You will need a chair, two sticks about the length of a hockey stick and two pieces of blue material about 1m x 2m. Optional extras are small, striped red teacloths as headgear for the Hebrew slaves and gold card circlets as headbands for the soldiers. Swords are not a good idea: imaginary ones are far more terrifying.

For this story you need a hero (choose a Moses and give her or him one stick). You also need a villain (choose a Pharaoh, sit her or him on a chair and give her or him the other stick as a sceptre). You need people to operate the scenery (spread out the blue cloths side by side and touching lengthways, and choose one person to hold each end of each piece—four people in all). Finally, you need everyone else to choose either to be poor downtrodden slaves (send them to sit by Moses) or to be Pharaoh's soldiers (send them to stand behind Pharaoh with their arms folded and with mean expressions on their faces).

Now, as a leader tells the story, the children should act it out.

Oh! *(Drop to your knees)* We were miserable! We Hebrews had been slaves in Egypt for three hundred years! We had to work for the rotten old Egyptians *(shake your fists at Pharaoh and his soldiers)* in their brickworks. We had to mix up sand and mud and straw *(do these actions and encourage the Hebrews to copy you)* and mould it into bricks and bake it— all in the scorching heat of the sun. And all so that the rotten old Egyptians could build their pyramids! Boo! *(Shake fists again)* We were so miserable, we groaned at God *(groan)*.

One day, when the time was right, God heard our groaning and he sent his friend Moses to rescue us from the Egyptians. Moses went to Pharaoh and said, 'God says, "Let my people go!"' *(Get Moses to say this)* But Pharaoh said, 'NO!' *(Get Pharaoh to say 'NO!' now and in the rest of this part of the story)* Moses went to Pharaoh many times and said, 'God says, "Let my people go!"' but each time Pharaoh said, 'NO!'

God sent terrible things on the Egyptians to make Pharaoh change his mind, but each time Pharaoh said

'NO!' In the end, God sent something so terrible—he killed the eldest child of all the Egyptians—that Pharaoh shouted, 'GET OUT!'

Moses led the people out of Egypt across the desert to the shores of the Red Sea. *(Plod across the room with the Hebrews to the edge of the sea)* And because they couldn't go any further, they set up camp. But, oh horrors! Oh terror! What should they see in the distance but the mighty Egyptian army! Pharaoh had changed his mind about letting them go, and there in the distance *(the soldiers come marching in slow motion)* were the terrifying Egyptians coming towards us, in their chariots with their swords glinting in the sunshine.

We moaned at God *(moan)* and we groaned at Moses *(groan)* and we said, 'If we were going to die, why couldn't we have died in Egypt without coming all this way?' But Moses trusted God. He stretched out his stick across the Red Sea and we watched in amazement as God made the waters part, making a dry path down the middle! *(The two sides of the sea are lifted and held vertically to make two walls with a path between them)* We set out as fast as we could towards the other side and freedom. The Egyptians came after us! *(The soldiers move closer in slow motion, pausing in the middle of the sea)* But, just as all the Hebrews reached the far side and freedom, Moses stretched out his stick again… and God made the waters of the Red Sea crash down on the Egyptians, washing them all away! *(You may not get to the end of this sentence as the sea will have got the idea and will have covered the Egyptians, who will drown)*

Moses had brought the people out of slavery to freedom, out of darkness to light. *(All cheer)*

## Footrest

Take a break here, with a drink and a biscuit for everyone.

## Footprints

For the next section of the programme, the children have the opportunity to experience two or three short workshops, depending on the time available. There are outlines for a drama activity (Footlights), a music workshop (Footnotes) and some craft ideas (Fancy footwork).

### Footlights

For this drama workshop, begin by exploring the difference between being in the light and being in the dark. For example, ask the group to imagine they are deep in an underground cave system. They can't see a thing (they could shut their eyes to help them into the scene). Slowly, they work their way along, feeling the rock wall and testing the ground carefully for hidden holes or obstacles. Have them work at this for a while and then suddenly call out 'lights', which is the signal that they can see clearly now. What do they see? Give them the opportunity to describe the imaginary scene before them.

Repeat this exercise with some other 'darkness into light' scenarios, such as being burglars breaking into a toy factory at night, walking through an eerie forest in deep darkness, sneaking into a dark kitchen to get a midnight snack when everyone is asleep, and so on.

What a difference light makes! It chases away the darkness. This is what God's light does, and he offers us a share in his powerful light. Talk through the following outline of how the story of Moses and God's people continues, with a view to acting it out in groups.

The people of God were rescued from slavery and God's light continued to lead them as they made their way back to the mountain where God had first called Moses from a bush—the bush that had burned with a light that would not go out—God's light.

God's light led them as a cloud by day and as fire by night. Finally, it settled over the special mountain, with lightning and fire. It was frightening. Only Moses could go close and climb the mountain to meet with God. He was away for a very long time but eventually he returned with the Ten Commandments. These were God's rules about how to be people through whom God's light could shine. Once, when Moses came down from that mountain, his face was shining so much with the special light from God that people couldn't even look at him without hurting their eyes. This was the light that beats all darkness.

Talk through the sort of things the people said about this light as they travelled, as they came close to the special mountain, as they waited for Moses, and finally when they saw him come down, glowing for God. Now divide the group up and ask them to work out a short scene around a tent in the desert as they discuss the strange events that they have seen and try to work out what it all means. End the scene when they suddenly see Moses and react to God's light shining from him.

## Footnotes

Many songs and hymns pick up the theme of light: some suggestions are given below. The music workshop could focus on learning to sing and accompany some of them. Beforehand, however, try experimenting with some instruments, using deep, low notes and sounds to represent darkness and higher notes to represent light. What might light 'beating' the darkness sound like? What sort of music would represent 'lighting up the dark'?

Suitable songs might include:

Keep a light in your eyes (*Big Blue Planet*)
Like a candle flame, flickering small (*Mission Praise* 420)
The light of Christ has come into the world (*Mission Praise* 652)

Light has dawned (*Mission Praise* 422)

Colours of day (*Junior Praise* 28)

Give me oil in my lamp (*Junior Praise* 50)

I am a lighthouse, a shining and bright house (*Junior Praise* 87)

Jesus bids us shine (*Junior Praise* 128)

Keep me shining, Lord (*Junior Praise* 147)

Rise, and shine and give God the glory (chorus only) (*Junior Praise* 210)

This little light of mine (*Junior Praise* 258)

## Fancy footwork

A number of craft activities work well with this theme, such as decorating candle holders or lanterns, creating coloured filters to cover torches, or designing 'stained-glass' windows using coloured acetate pieces. Further ideas can also be found in the *Make & Do* series published by *Barnabas* (see page 232 for details). Below are ideas for two lamps that you could make to light up the dark.

### A glow lamp

You will need a sheet of A4 dark-coloured paper cut in half lengthways, white tissue paper, scissors, glue sticks, felt pens, a glass jar and a small tealight.

Fold the dark-coloured paper in half many times along its width. Cut out triangles along the folded sides and then open out the paper. Glue tissue paper on to one side of the cut-out paper, covering all the cut-out areas. Colour the tissue over the cut-outs with felt pens. Roll the paper around the jar with the tissue paper layer underneath, and glue the ends together. Place a tealight candle inside the jar. Ask an adult to light the tealight with a taper.

## A paper lantern

You will need some coloured paper, some darker coloured card, scissors, glue sticks, a paper punch and coloured string.

Cut out two darker coloured strips of card as long as your sheet of coloured paper. Glue these strips to the top and bottom long edges of your coloured paper. Fold the paper in half along its length and make a sharp crease. Cut slits into the folded edge, up to the strips of card. Open out the paper.

Roll the paper and glue it along the short edges to form the lantern. Punch two holes, opposite one another, in one of the card strips. Tie coloured string into the holes and hang the lantern up. An additional feature would be to make an imitation flame from tissue paper, which you could stick (using double-sided tape) on to a circle of card at the bottom of the lantern. This gives the impression of a light burning inside the lantern.

## Foothold

Use today's chant (see above) to move on to a final time of worship together. The children should be in their groups. Each leader should be responsible for laying out a round piece of black felt in the centre of the circle of children, followed by a small white felt circle at the centre of the black piece, and finally a candle on the white circle. The candle is lit while the following words are said.

**Leader:** Today's story for the feast of All Saints has been about the battle between light and dark. Moses encountered God's light and he took that light down into the darkness of slavery to rescue

God's people. God's light is stronger than the darkness.

*Now tell the following story from the Bible, which is framed in terms of the struggle between light and dark. Whenever the word* dark *or* darkness *is heard, the children should cover their faces and close their eyes; whenever* light *is mentioned, they should move their hands away and look open-eyed toward the candle flame.*

**Leader:** In the beginning the world was *dark*, but then God said, 'Let there be *light!*' and the world changed from *darkness* to *light*. God divided the *light* from the *darkness* and called one 'day' (that was *light*) and the other 'night' (that was *dark*). God wanted all people to share his *light*. But God's people went through a very *dark* time when they were slaves in Egypt. So God rescued them and, when they had crossed the Red Sea with Moses, their hearts were full of *light*.

God led his people across the desert into freedom, and guided them with a *dark* pillar of cloud in the day time and a *light* fiery pillar in the night time, until they reached the place where he wanted them to live. Some of God's kings brought God's *light* and joy and peace to his people, but some brought *darkness* and sadness and pain.

God wanted everyone in the world to share his *light*. So he told the prophets to tell all

175

the people living in *darkness* that they could see God's *light* too. And one *dark* night, God's *light* came into the world in the shape of a baby. Jesus was born in the *darkness* of a stable and under the *light* of a star. When Jesus grew up, he turned the *darkness* of pain and suffering into the *light* of healing. He turned the *darkness* of loneliness into the *light* of being friends with God and with other people. Jesus turned the *darkness* of being confused into the *light* of understanding.

When Jesus died on the cross, the whole world went *dark*, but when he came back to life on Easter Sunday, the world was filled with *light* that shines on and on and on, and nothing will ever stop it shining. The *light* keeps shining in the *darkness* and the *darkness* has not put it out.

God calls each of us, just as he called Moses. He wants us all to *light* up the *dark*! *(Encourage the children to echo this.)* Light up the *dark*!

## Footsteps to the feast

To finish the session, use the footsteps chant to march everyone into a huge circle.

For the final game, you will need to buy several packs of the glow-in-the-dark stars that absorb light in the day time and give it off luminously at night. There needs to be at least one star for each person present. As you hold hands in the circle, remind everyone that God's light is offered to us as a gift through Jesus, who is the light for the world. God's saints can be any of his people who let that light shine in the darkness for him.

Invite everyone in the circle to receive one star from the leader nearest to them. Each leader should have a pack ready. Dim the artificial lights or daylight as much as possible and then link arms at the elbows, so that everyone's hands are free to hold the star in front of their bodies and create a circle of shining people who 'light up the dark'. An alternative to using the stars would be light sticks that glow when snapped. These lights will usually last for up to twelve hours.

## Stepping out

Finish the celebration of the feast with some food together, inviting parents and carers to join in. You could have some special biscuits or cakes on the theme, using dark and light chocolate, dark and light icing on digestive biscuits, or pieces of marble cake, made by adding cocoa to half the cake mix and then baking a dollop of light and dark mixture side by side.

# 11

# God's messengers!

## A special event for the feast of St Michael and All Angels

In former times, the Christian Church celebrated the feast of Michaelmas (St Michael and All Angels) more widely on 29 September. Today this festival is less well known, particularly in the Protestant world. In contrast, however, outside the church there is a growing interest in angels and their work. This may be one expression of today's spiritual climate, which instinctively recognizes and longs for a spiritual dimension to life, while wishing to keep it separate from the institution and apparatus of the traditional Church.

This hunger, which many feel the Christian faith does not fully satisfy, challenges those of us who are Christians about how we proclaim the true mystery of our faith. Our innate spirituality, with its awareness of something beyond the senses, is often more clearly experienced by children than by adults, so it is vital that we don't leave out or play down the supernatural parts of our story, such as the existence and work of angels. The aim of this outline is to celebrate their work and their part in the unfolding story of grace, as recorded in the Bible.

From fierce battle troopers in heaven's armies to tender protectors of God's people, and from awesome messengers of the good news to secret agents in the ordinary events of our lives, angels play a prominent part in the story of scripture. Jesus himself assures us that each of his little ones—the very children with whom we work—has his or her own guardian angel who always has direct access to God on their behalf (Matthew 18:10). So don't be surprised if one of the side-effects of this programme is that the children share their own stories of angels protecting and reassuring them. It was the experience of Christians in New Testament times, too. For example, Paul talks of an angel coming to comfort him (Acts 27:23) and Jesus himself was strengthened by angels after his time in the desert (Matthew 4:11).

Belief in angels is not an optional extra for Christians. We keep tumbling across them throughout the Bible. As the writer to the Hebrews reminds us, they are God's 'wind' and 'flaming fire' (Hebrews 1:7) and are constantly at work behind the scenes of our earthly lives, as well as looking on in amazement at the way God's grace is worked out in the lives of people who put their trust in Christ (1 Peter 1:12).

It is also important to establish at the outset that angels are not, according to the Bible, the cosy winged cherubs that we often see in paintings and clip art. Whenever they appear, they almost always have to tell people not to be afraid, which suggests that they are far from cuddly and cute. C.S. Lewis, in his science-fiction fantasy *Out of the Silent Planet*, paints a much more breathtaking picture of these awesome heavenly creatures in his description of the archangels who guard the planets.

The following outline focuses on some of the appearances of angels throughout the Old Testament in particular. Led by Archangel Michael, God's warrior angel, and Gabriel, God's messenger angel, there are literally hosts of angels at work within the stories of the patriarchs, priests and prophets. This programme also includes a reflective storytelling presentation from the Psalms, where the work of angels is described, as well as focusing for its central story on the angels who came to the rescue in the lives of Daniel and his friends.

## Bible footsteps

The key passage underpinning biblical stories about angels can be found in Hebrews 1:1–7.

## First steps

As the children and adults arrive, organize them into four or more groups, depending on numbers. These teams could be given names that reflect the different tasks of the heavenly host: for example, Warriors, Messengers, Singers, Protectors, Secret Agents, Guides.

An opening activity in groups could include creating a team banner decorated with the name of the team, using an angel template in various silver, yellow and gold shades. An older group might also like to cut out the outline of their team name from some black card, which they could then back with silver, yellow or gold so that the name shines through.

Each of these different angel groups should also be linked to a relevant Old Testament story, which the groups can begin to illustrate now, and later in the craft sessions. The illustrations could be drawn on to a length of blank wallpaper as a frieze beneath the banner. Each of the following stories will also form the basis for a group 'angel drama' later in the programme. For example:

- **Warriors:** The story of how horse-riding and chariot-driving angels appear on the hillsides surrounding Elisha and his servant at Dothan, when they are threatened by the king of Syria (see 2 Kings 6:11–23). Key verse: '"Don't be afraid," Elisha answered. "There are more troops on our side than on theirs"' (v. 16).
- **Messengers:** The story of when three angels visited Abraham and Sarah in the desert and announced that this elderly couple

would have a son (see Genesis 18:1–16.) Key verse: 'I am the Lord! There is nothing too difficult for me' (v. 14).

☺ **Singers:** The story of Isaiah's vision in the temple, when he saw angels calling to each other about the holiness of God. Their voices shook the whole building and caused Isaiah to fall on his knees in worship (see Isaiah 6:1–8). Key verse: 'Holy, holy, holy, Lord All-Powerful! The earth is filled with your glory' (v. 3).

☺ **Protectors:** The story of the angels who saw off the invading Assyrian armies encamped under the very walls of Jerusalem (see 2 Chronicles 32:1–23). Key verse: 'Hezekiah and the prophet Isaiah son of Amoz asked the Lord for help, and he sent an angel who killed every soldier and commander in the Assyrian camp' (vv. 20–21).

☺ **Secret agents:** The writer to the Hebrews assures us that we need to be on the alert because, in welcoming outsiders, we may be entertaining angels without realizing it (Hebrews 13:2). It seems that angels can sometimes appear as human beings, which means, of course, that they are in disguise for our good. Sometimes people do not recognize them as angels, such as when Balaam on his donkey failed to notice the angel in front of him. The animal, however, was not so blind and eventually God spoke through the mouth of the animal to alert Balaam to the presence of God's angel (see Numbers 22:21–35). Key verse: 'Balaam lost his temper, then picked up a stick and hit the donkey. When that happened, the Lord told the donkey to speak' (vv. 27–28).

☺ **Guides:** The story of when an angel showed Moses and the Israelites the way out of Egypt during the story of the exodus. The angel appeared in a pillar of cloud by day and a pillar of fire by night (see Exodus 13:21–22; 14:19–20). Key verse: 'All this time God's angel had gone ahead of Israel's army, but now he moved behind them' (14:19).

## Footsteps chant

Here is a simple chant that you could use with the children at various points during the day as a transition between activities. Start a simple clapping rhythm and then call out each line for the children to echo.

> *We're on an angel journey*
> *Of flame and wind and wing,*
> *To see how God looks after us*
> *As children of the king.*

## First footing

Gather the children together and introduce the angel theme by teaching some lively actions for each of the ways God sends angels to work alongside us. For example:

- ❂ **As warriors:** brandishing a pretend sword (like a lightsabre) with swishing noises.
- ❂ **As messengers:** blowing a trumpet with appropriate noises.
- ❂ **As singers:** on tiptoes, hitting and sustaining as high a note as possible for a count of ten.
- ❂ **As protectors:** sweeping arms from side to front as if covering something or someone under wings, whistling gently.
- ❂ **As secret agents:** hunching shoulders, pretending to have up-turned collars, and moving around the room furtively, humming the *Pink Panther* tune.
- ❂ **As guides:** wagging a finger as if to say 'Not this way' (accompanied by a negative 'uh-uh'), and then pointing in another direction.

Play around with the different command words to change the actions and sounds in rapid succession.

Explain to the children that God has an army of helpers available to help us in the battle with all that is bad. His angels are his messengers, guides, protectors and secret agents on earth. According to some descriptions of angels in the Bible, they are very large, supernatural winged beings that are very scary, but the good news is that they are on our side. Today's feast is celebrating St Michael, who is one of the chief angels (an archangel) along with all the others who appear in the stories in the Bible.

Today's story is about Daniel and his friends and how angels intervened to save them from roaring flames and roaring lions.

## Footbridge

An angel appeared in the fiery furnace with Daniel's three friends, protecting them from the fierce heat surrounding them. Perhaps the angel's own fiery flame was able to cancel out the hothouse temperature of the furnace.

Play a game together in which one of the teams becomes the king and Daniel's enemies, while the others are Daniel's friends on the run. As soon as anyone is tagged, they must be taken to one of four cardboard bases around the edge of your playing area (made of opened-out and flattened cardboard boxes). The only way they can be released is if three others from their team come and stand with the captured person on the card square for a count of ten. Once the four have been there for that length of time, they are free to go. Daniel's friends stayed together and, with an angel's help, they were saved from their enemies. Position a leader by each of the cardboard squares to check that the escape rules are obeyed.

An angel also appears in the story of Daniel, when he was thrown into the lions' den. This angel shut the lions' mouths so that they did not harm him. Play a team game of 'still lions', in which the children should prowl and roar their way around the room until the leader (the angel) calls out 'mouths shut', at which they should all freeze on the spot. Which team can maintain the stillest pride of lions for longest?

## Best foot forward

The following stories about Daniel and his friends come from Daniel 3 and 6. Tell the stories to the whole group. Beforehand, teach the following words or sounds and actions to the children, which they should contribute whenever those particular words are mentioned in your retelling.

- **King:** bow heads with the words 'Your Majesty'.
- **Soldiers:** marching sounds using feet or hands on the ground, with the words 'left-right, left-right'.
- **Instruments:** children should choose any instrument they like and mime playing it, making appropriate noises.
- **Golden statue:** look up high and say 'Wow!'
- **Leaders and officials:** salute and say, 'Yes, sir!'
- **Shadrach, Meshach, Abednego** and **Daniel:** hands raised and a cheer of 'Hurray!'
- **Fiery furnace:** hold out two hands as if in front of a fire, and say, 'Phew! That's hot!'
- **Angel:** make whooshing sound and call out, 'God to the rescue!'
- **Lions:** a hearty roar.

Practise the sounds and actions several times and then start the story below, cueing in the responses to the key words.

God's people had been taken far away from their home and were now living in the city of Babylon. The **king** of Babylon was all-powerful; he had a great army of **soldiers** and many **leaders and officials**. The **king** needed to make sure he kept good control. He decided to test the loyalty of his **leaders and officials** by building a huge **golden statue**. The **king** commanded all the **leaders and officials** to bow down to the **golden statue** whenever all the royal **instruments** were played (horns, pipes, lyres, trumpets, harps and bagpipes).

Now, among the **leaders and officials** were the three friends of **Daniel**. Their names were **Shadrach, Meshach and Abednego**. They were part of God's people from Jerusalem and worshipped the one true God. They could not, and would not, bow down to the **golden statue**. So, when all the **instruments** sounded, the **king** was angry to see that **Shadrach, Meshach and Abednego** would not bow down.

He sent his **soldiers** to take **Shadrach, Meshach and Abednego** prisoner. 'Why don't you bow down to the **golden statue**?' the **king** asked. **Shadrach, Meshach and Abednego** replied, 'Because we serve the one true God.' 'Then you must be punished for disobeying,' said the **king**. The **soldiers** took **Shadrach, Meshach and Abednego** to the **fiery furnace**, but the three friends were not afraid. Whether God rescued them or not, they would not be unfaithful to him. The **king** threw the three men into the **fiery furnace**. Everyone held their breath. Everyone expected to see a grisly sight, as **Shadrach Meshach and Abednego** burned. But, when the **king** looked into the **fiery furnace**, he saw not three men, but four. God had sent an **angel** to be with them.

**Shadrach, Meshach and Abednego** were safe! The **king** was amazed. He brought them out of the **fiery furnace**: God had kept them safe using his **angel**. The **king** now knew that there was someone greater than him. He decided that he would serve the same God as **Shadrach, Meshach and Abednego**.

Many years later under a new **king**, new **leaders and officials** tried to trick **Daniel** in the same way. The new **king**'s officers and leaders were jealous of **Daniel** because he was successful. God had given him wisdom and **Daniel** had become the leading adviser in the country. The **leaders and officials** plotted to trap the **king** into getting rid of **Daniel**. They made him sign an order that no one was to pray to anyone but him. **Daniel** could not do this: he served the one true God.

The **leaders and officials** brought **Daniel** to the **king**, explaining that he had disobeyed the law. The **king** realized that he had been tricked but he could not change his law, so the **king** had to throw **Daniel** into the den of **lions**. Everyone held their breath. Everyone expected to see an even more grisly thing happen to **Daniel**. But the next morning, when the **king** called **Daniel**, he said, 'Here I am, safe and sound. God has sent his **angel** to shut up the mouths of the **lions**.' This **king**, too, decided that **Daniel**'s God was the one true God and began to worship him. God's **angel** had shown that God was truly a rescuing God.

### Footrest

At this point, take a break for a drink and a biscuit in each angel team area. Those who finish quickly could continue their angel story frieze and finish decorating their team space (see 'First steps' on pages 180–181).

# Footprints

Each group should now have a chance to experience one or more of the following three activity sessions, moving from one to the other either as a single angel group or, if you have six groups, two angel groups together.

## Footlights

The focus for this drama workshop will be acting out one or both angel stories linked to each group (see 'First steps' on pages 180–181).

As a warm-up, have the children perform some 'angel' star-jumps, followed by modelling various flying positions. They can also practise tiptoeing their way around the room and then, on the word 'look' from the leader, freezing in a sudden dramatic pose (hands held high and on tiptoes), saying in unison, 'Do not be afraid!'

Run through the angel story (or stories) that you will be doing with the group. (For a suggestion of appropriate stories, see the summary and Bible references in 'First steps'). Now focus on one scene from the story, asking the children to think of all the people, angels, objects and even animals that could be involved in this part of the drama. Then ask the children to create a freeze-frame of that one scene, taking the parts of everything there, animate and inanimate. Once you have satisfactorily created this photo-moment from the story, you could proceed in one of two ways, depending on the age level of your group.

1. Work out one simple action or sound that each person in the scene can perform, and have a leader (or perhaps an older child) as the director, who will decide in which order everything will happen. You could take this further, asking the children to work out one spoken line that they might be saying in this freeze-frame. Again, the director will need to help put these words in

order. Rehearse the whole scene together, perhaps with a view to showing it as a presentation to the others at the end of the programme.

2. Alternatively, ask the children to think of the 'before' and 'after' of this scene. How did everything and everybody arrive in this position? With a little guidance, older groups will be able to work out some simple dialogue and actions that allow them to arrive at the frozen moment that they have just rehearsed, and take it on afterwards. Rehearse the scene, perhaps to use in a presentation to the others at the end of the programme.

## Footnotes

Provide a box of percussion instruments, asking the children to experiment with the sort of sounds that angels might make when they appear on earth. For example, the rushing wind as they fly on to the scene, the rustle of their wings, the commanding sound of a powerful voice, the harmony of their singing, and so on. (**NB:** In some Orthodox liturgies, small, delicate cymbals are regularly shaken to imitate the sound of the fluttering wings of the cherubim.)

Angels are given to much singing in the Bible, particularly around the miracle of Christmas and in John's account of heaven in the book of Revelation. The psalmists encourage the angels to praise the Lord (Psalm 103:20; 148:2) and the angels' favourite song seems to be one about how special God is, namely, 'Holy, holy, holy is the Lord God Almighty.'

There are several versions of this song that you could teach the children, probably choosing just one verse in particular to practise. For example:

Holy, holy, holy, Lord God Almighty (*Mission Praise* 237)
Holy, holy, holy is the Lord (*Mission Praise* 239)
Glory, glory in the highest (*Mission Praise* 174) You could substitute the word 'holy' for 'glory' and sing 'holy is the Lamb'.

'We see the Lord' (*Mission Praise* 736) is a musical version of the story of how Isaiah saw angels singing in the temple (Isaiah 6:1–8). The words could be changed to 'He sees the Lord'. There is plenty of scope here for a dramatic percussion build-up as the song progresses.

## Fancy footwork

There are various ways to make model angels or angel costumes that the children could take home. Some of them are set out more fully in other Barnabas books. For example, in *Story Plays for Christmas* by Vicki Howie, there are instructions for making angel wings, as follows.

Take one large piece of good-quality gold or silver card. Fold in half and draw the shape of an angel's wing. Cut out the shape and open it up. Make two small holes in the middle section of the wings and thread through lengths of gold or silver tinsel. Wrap the tinsel around the angel to keep the wings in shape. Alternatively, net curtains, gathered in the middle, sewn on to the back of a tunic and attached to the angel's wrists, make very effective 'floaty' wings. Unwanted CDs sewn on to the angel's costume are also very effective. Look out for and save the free ones!

In *Step-by-Step Christmas Crib* by Leena Lane and Gillian Chapman, there are instructions for making mini angels, as follows.

You will need long craft pipe cleaners, scraps of white fabric, yarn, a small wooden bead, gold thread and thin coloured card. Make a body shape (but no legs) from the pipe cleaner and use the small bead to become the head. Wrap white yarn around the arms and roll the card to become the main body. Cut short lengths of brown yarn for the angel's hair that you stick to the bead. For a robe, use a rectangle of white fabric, in which you cut a hole for the head and then push it down over the body. Cut out some silver paper wings and add some gold yarn for the belt. Paint on a face to the bead.

From *Christmas Make & Do* by Gillian Chapman, there are instructions for making pop-up angel cards, as follows. You can illustrate the cards with the key verse from the angel story appropriate to each group (see 'First steps' on pages 180–181).

Fold a piece of A5 card in half, crease and open out. Cut out a strip of card (3cm times 15cm), fold it in half and crease the centre fold. Fold down the two ends of the strip and stick them to the inside of the first piece of card, ensuring that the centre creases in both card and strip match exactly. Make an angel by sticking together a triangular card shape for the body, an oval for the face, plus arms and wing shapes. Add golden thread for hair. Fold the angel in half, creasing firmly. Then stick the angel to the card strip, ensuring that the centre creases in both strip and angel fit exactly. The angel should fold up as you close the card flat; when you open the card again, the angel should pop forward.

Finally, from *Advent Angels* by Sue Doggett, there are instructions for making an angel decoration, as follows.

Fold a piece of A4 card in half and trace a basic (bell) angel shape on one side. Take six pieces of paper (silver, gold and white) and fold each one in half and in half again. Trace the basic bell-shape of the angel on to each piece of paper, cut out this shape and then open them out into two piles, with four of each colour in each pile. Fold and interleaf the colours. Staple the shapes together along the fold. Now stick one half of the bell shape on to the angel on the card, linking the different pleats of the bell-shape with some double-sided tape. Do the same with the second half of the bell-shaped pieces. Add some angel hair. The angel's body should now be like a frilly bell decoration.

## Foothold

One of the Bible's most dramatic encounters with an angel was experienced by Jacob, who, in a dream, saw a host of them going up and down a ladder linking earth and heaven (see Genesis 28:12). It seems that angels are busy beings, always active for God in this world. Jacob also had a wrestling match with an angel, but that's another story (see Genesis 32:22–32).

As a way of bringing the programme to a prayerful end, ask the children to gather in their angel teams in a circle. At the centre of each circle, a leader should place a stone. The following words can be read centrally by one leader for the whole event, while the objects are placed and actions are performed within the groups.

**Leader:** Angels are all around us, even though we don't see them. Jacob once discovered this. He was in trouble at home and had run away. He had to sleep rough in the open. He even had to use a stone as a pillow. As he dozed, suddenly he saw a ladder reaching up to heaven from where he lay.

*Introduce a crafted ladder made from several long drinking straws.*

**Leader:** On the ladder he saw angels going up and down, doing God's work. God had not abandoned him.

*For angels, have prepared a large number of shiny silver triangle shapes. The leader should stick two of them on to the straw ladder with some sticky fixers and then invite the group prayerfully to add more angels on to the ladder, prompted by the following words.*

**Leader:** God has appointed a guardian angel to watch over each one of us.

*Each child should stick on one angel to remind them of this truth.*

Reproduced with permission from *Footsteps to the Feast* published by BRF 2007 (978 1 84101 464 7).

**Leader:** God uses his angels to protect those we love.

*Each child should stick another angel on the ladder to remind them of this wonderful truth.*

**Leader:** God has a message for each one of us, because there's something special he has called each of us to do in the work of heaven and earth.

*Each child should stick a final angel on to the ladder in response to this amazing truth. Pause for a moment to enjoy the ladder full of angels! Finish with the following prayer together.*

**All:** Thank you, Father, that your angels are busy at work all around us, helping us to love and serve you. Help us to hear the messages they bring, to join in with their praise, to experience their protection and to follow their guidance, for your name's sake. Amen

## Footsteps to the feast

Use the chant (see page 182) to gather the children into a large circle for the final part of the programme. Do you know what makes the angels really happy? According to Jesus, it is when you and I decide to say 'yes' to God and follow him (see Luke 15:10). You might say it sends them into cartwheels of joy and somersaults of praise! They know how important each one of us is to God, and how much God loves us and wants us to be his friends.

Set the circle swirling with joy in the following way. The leader should start by turning to the child on his or her left. Leader and child reach out their right hands to hold on to each other as they turn in a circle on the spot, swapping places. Each now does the same with the people next to them so that, one by one, everyone starts twirling and shaking hands in a great cartwheel of joy.

## Stepping out

Invite parents and carers to join you for a feast together. Angel cake should surely be on the menu for today!

# 12

# Read all about it!

## A special event to celebrate Bible Sunday

Though not strictly one of the great feasts of the Church, Bible Sunday is a special day in the year. It celebrates the gift of the word of God, which, as the traditional Collect for this day prays, Christians should 'read, mark, learn and inwardly digest'. The Bible is the Christian's special book. It is the story of how God has spoken to people and revealed his character of purity and love. Christians believe that it is inspired by God (see 2 Timothy 3:16) and is alive with the truth about God and our human nature. From its stories they learn how to follow God's ways more faithfully, and through its verses Christians can hear God speaking to them today. As the apostle Paul writes, 'The Scriptures were written to teach and encourage us by giving us hope' (Romans 15:4).

Outside the Church, however, these inspired stories are less well known. It should come as no surprise that the Bible is kept back for the higher-value questions in TV quiz shows! Even among Christians, there is a danger that only certain favourite bits of the Bible are known, while the bigger picture of how it all fits together and the place of individual stories in the grand scheme of God's great rescue plan for the world is not well understood. Sunday group teaching programmes often contribute to this lack of under-standing, moving rather randomly from episode to episode in the Bible in an unconnected way. Paul tells us that God sent Jesus 'when the time was right' (Galatians 4:4). This means that the story of Jesus, so important to us as Christians, comes from within a greater context; if we don't know that context, we may miss much of the wonder and significance of what God has done.

This programme seeks to celebrate the wholeness and interconnectedness of our sacred book. It aims to celebrate the diversity of its contents while tracing the unfolding pattern of grace that threads throughout its stories. It can be used at any time of the year, although, traditionally, Bible Sunday fell in Advent. In more recent years it has been celebrated in October.

## Bible footsteps

The Bible is the big story. We bring our own individual stories to it, so that through this encounter we might discover new things about God and ourselves on our journey of faith. As the writer of Psalm 119 reminds us, in his majestic poem all about God's written revelation, 'Your word is a lamp that gives light wherever I walk' (Psalm 119:105). Earlier in that same psalm, he prays, 'Open my mind and let me discover the wonders of your Law' (v. 18).

## First steps

As the children arrive and after they have been registered, invite everyone to join teams, which take on the names of items linked to books—for example, Chapters, Verses, Paragraphs, Contents, Index, Pages and so on. Each team area should have a simple wooden bookshelf available, ideally with five separate shelves, which will gradually be filled to make a Bible library. Have available at each team base a variety of differently coloured card, which the teams can make into new book covers to cover ordinary books that have been collected at each station. Each team will need 66 books to recover! When the books are recovered, they should be stacked on the shelves to become the books of the Bible. Here is a possible colour scheme:

## Old Testament

- Five books of the law in green (Genesis to Deuteronomy)
- Twelve history books in red (Joshua to Esther)
- Six poetry and wisdom books in yellow (Job to Song of Songs, plus Lamentations)
- Sixteen books of prophecy in purple (Isaiah, Jeremiah and Ezekiel to Malachi)

## New Testament

- Four Gospels in white (Matthew to John)
- One history book in red (Acts)
- Twenty-one letters in blue (Romans to Jude)
- One book of prophecy in purple (Revelation)

As each book is covered, arrange them on the Bible bookshelf as a visual demonstration of the variety of literature within God's special book. This activity could be continued at other times throughout the event and the teams might like to add the names of the books along the spines. You could also decorate the team bases with a variety of versions of the Bible, including some with colour illustrations—both elaborate illuminated versions from the past and modern examples.

Once all have arrived, gather everyone together to introduce the day. Begin by using the following Bible workout, using activities and actions to go alongside the different books of the Bible.

Start the session by asking each person in the group to find a space of their own around the room.

Now ask the group to follow the actions mimed by the leader. The leader should mime the opening of a big book… turning its pages… finding the right chapter (*move your pointed finger along and down imaginary columns*), marking a particular verse… reading the line (*exaggerate the head and eye movement for this*), a pause to think (*finger on chin*), a pause to pray (*hands together*), more reading…

another pause to think... another short prayer... the closing of the book... finishing with a big sigh.

Ask the group what they thought you as leader were doing. Move on to ask what their favourite book is. Tell them that, for Christians, the Bible is a special favourite book to be read thoughtfully and prayerfully, as it is one way in which they hear God speaking. The group are now going to explore this book in actions.

The group should be standing ready for the following fast-moving, physical exploration of the Bible. They should copy the leader's workout actions.

- Run on the spot with 33 quick double steps (1-2,1-2,1-2 and so on, to demonstrate that the Bible has 66 books.
- Sweep your right arm out from your side, all the way to above your head. Sweep your left arm out from your side to above your head, to demonstrate that the Bible has two halves; the Old and New Testament.
- Use one arm and then the other to imitate the clock hand ticking its way around the clock face that is your body. Count in hundreds up to 1000 on one half of the clock face and another 1000 on the other half, to demonstrate that the Bible records about 2000 years of history.
- Stand like a comic policeman with hands behind back and do five knee bends. There are five books of the law (use words, too, such as 'hello, hello, hello, hello, hello', and, the second time you do it, 'Abraham, Isaac, Jacob, Joseph, Moses'). These books are in the Old Testament (sweep right hand out from your side as described above).
- Next we get down on one knee, as if before a king or honoured leader. There are twelve books of history about kings, judges and special leaders. Bow down on one knee twelve times. These books are also in the Old Testament (sweep right hand out from side).
- There are also love stories, praise songs, wise sayings and sad poems in the Bible. For each of these words have a simple

action, such as touching the heart, lifting hands high, stroking your chin, rubbing tearful eyes. Repeat this a few times. There are six books like this in the Old Testament (sweep right hand out from side).

☼ Teach three actions: pointing forward with the words 'watch out'; one hand to one ear with the words 'listen up'; a hand shading your eyes as if looking into the distance with the words 'look forward'. There are 16 prophets who wrote books in the Bible telling God's people to watch out… listen up… look forward. Repeat this with words and actions 16 times! These books are also in the Old Testament (sweep right hand out from side).

☼ Stand to attention and then, on the spot, jump four quarter-turns to face left, back, right and front again, demonstrating that there are four books of stories about Jesus. As you jump round on the spot, recite 'Matthew, Mark, Luke and John'. Repeat this a few times. These books are in the New Testament (sweep left hand out from your side as described above).

☼ Now freeze in a dramatic pose to pause the action for a moment. There is one history book, called Acts, in the New Testament part of the Bible (after a while, unfreeze and sweep left hand out from side).

☼ Get ready for 21 star jumps, to look like a great capital 'X'. There are 21 letters written about God's love. Do 21 star jumps. These books are also in the New Testament (sweep left hand out from side).

☼ Finally, all lie down as if asleep and then stand up in slow motion and look as if you have seen something incredible! There is one final book… at the end… a special vision… a dream picture… full of mysteries… called Revelation. This book is about the end of this world and the beginning of heaven. It is in the New Testament (sweep left hand out from side).

☼ And that's the Bible—God's special book. All together, take a deep breath and then say 'Wow!'

What a book. If you have any energy left at the end, you could try doing all this again!

This book is special: it is the big story of God's love for his world. It begins with God making the world and ends with him making all things new. It starts in a glorious garden and ends in a magnificent city. It is all about people like you and me who put their trust in God. It is about journeys, battles, family disputes, joy and sadness. It is about Jesus—his birth, life, death and rising again. It is about how more and more people join God's family through Jesus. All life and eternal life is here! Today we shall be exploring this amazing book and how Christians come close to God through reading its stories.

## Footsteps chant

Teach the following rhyme to a simple clapping rhythm, with the children and adults echoing each line after the leader. Use this chant, varying the pitch and the volume, to accompany movement from one activity to another throughout the programme.

*We're on a special journey*
*Of stories from the Book.*
*To know God's love and what he's like,*
*It's here we're going to look.*

## First footing

This is an activity based on the game of Dingbats, in which famous words or phrases are disguised in a word puzzle. It gives a flavour of the range of stories, events and characters that are contained in God's special book.

You will need to explain the way these Biblebat word puzzles work, by showing a few examples, such as R/E/A/D/I/N/G = reading between the lines, and ᴘ ᴀ ɪ N S = growing pains. The following Biblebat puzzles should be enlarged and copied on to A4 or A3 paper, so that they can be pinned up around a room. Children could work in groups or together with adults and, if they have a Bible each, the contents page or index would be a useful place for them to find clues.

Here are some suggestions for three lists of Biblebats. The first is for Bible books, the second Bible characters and the third Bible events. The answers are listed at the end.

## Bible books

a) X

b) 7, 33, 15, 8, 41, 2…

c) George and Edward

d) Male makes tea

e) mouth $^{eyes}$ nose

f) 2 + 2 = 4; ~~S~~; U

g) Jeffreys and Dread

h) Teacher, builder, policeman…

i) scenes + scenes + scenes

j) knee $^{am}$

## Bible characters

a) m, n, o, p, q, s, t, u

b) $\pi$ unpunctual

c) GGGG us

d) the day before

e) (O2 N) ~~off~~

f) ɰ

g) Auction item

h) Jo's F

i) He saw

j) + am

## Bible events or places

a) water
   world
b) Biro T ££
c) ~~The Jordan~~
d)   O
     L I
     V E S
e) lionsdanielden
f) EgBA527ypt
g) A* YYY males
h) SPAAUULL
i) ~~Worl~~D
j) Ro~~man~~of

### Answers

Books: a) Mark; b) Numbers; c) 2 Kings; d) Hebrews; e) Isaiah;
f) Matthew; g) Judges; h) Job; i) Acts; j) Nehemiah (knee, am
higher)

Characters: a) Noah (no 'r'); b) Pilate; c) Jesus; d) Eve; e) Aaron;
f) Eli (E lie); g) Lot; h) Joseph; i) Esau; j) Adam

Events or places: a) the flood (world under water); b) Pentecost;
c) crossing of the Jordan; d) Mount of Olives; e) Daniel in the
lions' den; f) flight into Egypt; g) three wise men follow a star;
h) Saul's conversion; i) the end of the world; j) the lowering of the
man through the roof (to be healed by Jesus).

# Footbridge

Here are some simple book-related games to use with the group.

1. Play this adaptation of the 'fruit salad' game. Ask the children
to stand in a circle. Go round the circle giving the word 'chapter',

'verse' or 'book' to each member of the group. Then ask for a volunteer to stand in the middle. The volunteer is now without a place in the circle. When the leader calls out one of the three words, the children who have been given this word must quickly walk across the circle to stand on the opposite side. As this is happening, the volunteer in the middle should try to take up one of the empty spaces. The child who ends up without a space becomes the one in the middle. If the leader says 'Bible', all the children must move.

The basic format of this game works with any group of four related words, so you might like to invent some examples of your own, linked to the Bible.

**2.** Organize some relay races between teams, including the balancing of a book on the head of the runner each time.

**3.** Play a game of charades between teams in which one or two or more have to act out certain Bible stories. Can the other team guess which story it is? From the suggested list below, choose stories that you feel your groups will know well.

Noah's ark (Genesis 6:1—9:17); Joseph's special coat (Genesis 37:1–4); Crossing the Red Sea (Exodus 14:21–22); Moses receives the Ten Commandments (Exodus 19:16–25); Joshua and the walls of Jericho (Joshua 6:6–20); a Samson story (for example, from Judges 16:20); David and Goliath (1 Samuel 17:41–50); Jonah and the big fish (Jonah 1:13–17); Daniel and the lions' den (Daniel 6:1–23); Jesus' birth (Luke 2:1–7); Jesus walks on water (Mark 6:45–52); Jesus and Zacchaeus (Luke 19:1–10); Paul being shipwrecked (Acts 27:39–44).

**4.** This game is, again, open to endless variations for introducing key words, ideas and themes. Have the children stand in a circle, but all facing outwards. On a given signal, the children jump and turn so that the circle is facing inward. To activate this, the leader calls out a word and, on the count of three, everyone jumps and turns to mime their version of that word. Each child will then be 'frozen' in a particular mime, which they believe best illustrates it.

To connect the game with an understanding of the Bible, use words that describe different landscapes from the Bible, such as desert, mountaintop, seascape, busy city and so on. What sort of statues will the children create? You could try the different occupations of the authors of the various Bible books, such as soldier, priest, king, doctor, fisherman, scholar and so on—or different moods and activities from the Bible, such as romance, fear, sadness, celebration, fighting and travel. It is best to keep the signal to one simple word. You might like to try inventing some more key words of your own for the children to mime. You could introduce Bible characters if your group are familiar with them, or perhaps some Bible animals. The field is wide open!

## Best foot forward

For this presentation you need to study the Bible labyrinth template on page 229. This labyrinth is designed so that key Old and New Testament events are brought together at various points to help connect up the whole Bible story. You will need a large floor space to set this up, using masking tape and arranging the numbered areas in such a way that groups of six or seven children from one team can sit comfortably in a circle at each of the stations of the labyrinth. Ideally, the labyrinth needs to be set up in a separate space, in advance of the event.

When the children walk from one station to the next, they should do so in single file and use the footsteps chant (see page 199) as they move along. You also need one leader to bring up the rear of each group, as he or she will be responsible for rearranging anything that has been built or made at the station by the group that has just left, ready for the next group to arrive.

There are 13 stations in all. This is how they pair up:

1 and 13: Creation and new creation (with the theme of making).

2 and 12: Noah's ark and Holy Communion (with the theme of remembering).

3 and 11: The call of Abraham and the great commission (with the theme of calling).

4 and 10: The exodus and the Easter story (with the theme of rescuing).

5 and 9: The Ten Commandments and the Beatitudes (with the theme of receiving).

6 and 8: Entering the promised land and baptism (with the theme of entering).

7 alone: The incarnation—God becoming a human (with the theme of arriving).

At each station, there will be an activity and a brief retelling of the relevant Bible story. Each team should go round as a group, staggering the journeys through the Bible labyrinth so that there are at least two stations free between groups. Groups who are waiting to go could spend time completing their Bible library in their team base.

Here are the stories and activities at each station:

## 1: Creation

You will need a black circle of felt or cloth for the centre of this station, and six pieces of fabric coloured white, blue, green, yellow, grey and red, which form a hexagon shape when put together. You will build the hexagon as you tell the story. Finally, you will need a box full of items linked to creation, such as pictures of water, models of plants and trees, models of the sun, stars and moon, model fish, birds and animals, and some model human beings.

In the beginning God made the heaven and the earth. He began by saying, 'Let there be light' and there was light. *(Put down the white hexagon piece)* It was good. Next he made the water *(Put down the blue hexagon piece)*, and that too was good. Then God made the land *(Put down the green piece, building up the hexagon)*, and he saw that that was good. Next came the sun, moon and stars to give light for the day and the night. *(Put down the yellow piece)* This was good. Then he filled the waters with fish of all kinds, and the air with birds *(Put down the grey piece)*, and he said that that was good. Finally, he made the creatures *(Put down the red piece, completing the hexagon)*, and he also made people—you and me—and put us in charge of his world, to look after it.

Now invite the group to talk about which part of creation they like best. Then, from your box of objects, invite the children in turn to select items to place on the different colours of the hexagon. Finish by putting a candle on to the white piece, lighting it and saying, 'When God saw everything that he had made, he said it was very good. When he had finished creating the world, God rested.'

## 2: Noah's ark

You will need a circle of brown felt or cloth for the centre of this station of the labyrinth, a boat to represent the ark, some small golden stones to build an altar and several strips of fabric in the colours of the rainbow.

God made everything good, but soon the world began to go bad. People chose not to care for God's world or even for each other. God was sad and decided to start all over again by sending a flood. Only Noah's family truly believed in God, so they were kept safe in a boat called an ark. *(Lift up the ark as you say the next part)* On board were representatives of all the animals that God had made, so that God could fill his cleaned-up world with life again after the flood.

When the flood was over *(Lower the ark back on to the cloth)* Noah and his family and the animals came out. They remembered to thank God for all that he had done. *(Put down one golden stone to represent the altar. Now invite the children to add more stones to build the altar of thanks further. Ask them what sort of things they might thank God for. As they mention items, they add their stones.)*

Then God gave them a sign that he would never stop loving his world and its people in future. He gave them a rainbow.

Invite each child to take a piece of the fabric and together build a rainbow around the edge of the brown cloth, where the ark and altar are.

### 3: The call of Abraham

You will need a circle of sandy-coloured cloth or felt for the centre of this station of the labyrinth, and a set of fluorescent stars (at least two or three for every child).

God never stopped loving his people. He wanted to help them to trust him, whatever happened. Once, he spoke to a man called Abraham and told him and his wife Sarah to set out on a dangerous journey across the desert to a new place to live called Canaan. Abraham could not see God, but he believed that God was always close. God kept them safe on their long journey. *(As you say this, trace a twisty journey with your finger across the sandy-coloured base cloth.)* He then gave them a very special safe place to live. He also promised them that he would give them a son and that from this son would come a family and a great nation. In that nation one day a very special person would be born, who would bring God's love to the whole world. God's family would be world-big and contain as many people as there are stars in the sky or grains of sand in the desert. God kept his promise.

Invite the children to place their stars on to the sandy base cloth as you tell the last part of the story. As they put the stars down, invite them to name as many countries in the world as they can think of. God's family would be in every country one day.

## 4: The exodus

You will need a circle of green cloth or felt for this station of the labyrinth, as well as five pieces of wood of equal length, which together create a doorframe—two pieces for each side and one for the lintel—and three red circles which can fit on each side of the door and the lintel. (NB: a similar set of five pieces will be used at station 10 to create a cross). Finally, you will need some matzo bread in a basket.

God's people didn't find it easy to trust God. They often made mistakes and often deliberately chose to go their own way, ending up in trouble. Many, many years after Abraham, they were in Egypt as slaves. Their situation seemed hopeless but God did not forget them. He sent Moses to bring them to freedom. The Pharaoh in Egypt only let them go when a terrible thing happened: all the eldest boy children of the Egyptians, including the Pharaoh's own son, died. God's people, however, were kept safe because they had put lamb's blood around the doors of their houses. *(Create the door with the pieces of wood and add the red circles)* The angel of death had passed over them and they were saved. Moses led them across the Reed Sea to freedom.

They had been in such a rush to leave that there had been no time to bake proper bread for the journey. It had no yeast or leaven in it, so it was flat. They called it unleavened bread. Whenever they ate this bread, they remembered how God had rescued them from being slaves and brought them into freedom.

Share some matzo bread with the children. Can they taste the story?

### 5: The Ten Commandments

You will need a circle of grey cloth for this station of the labyrinth, a basket of small stones and some chalk (at least one stone and one piece of chalk for every child).

God guided Moses, and he led God's people through the desert to a new home. God gave them miracle food to eat and water to drink. But, even then, some of them began to doubt God's love. It was so easy to forget the best way to live, so God called Moses up a mountain and gave him the Ten Commandments. These ten rules would help people to know how to come close to God. They told the people how to love God and love other people. *(Use your fingers and thumbs as a quick way of going through the Ten Commandments briefly. For example, God is number one, his image is secret, his name is special, and his day is holy. Honour your parents, and don't break your marriage (link up the small fingers of both hands for these two commandments). Don't steal, don't murder, don't lie, don't want what others have.)*

I wonder what rules you would suggest for living the very best life you can? What key qualities are most important to God? Love? Kindness? Friendship? Discuss this briefly with the children. Then they can pick a stone on which to write the key quality that they think would please God most and help us to live well. Place the stones down in the shape of a heart on the grey cloth.

### 6: Entering the promised land

You will need a blue circle of felt or cloth for this station of the labyrinth, some small pieces of stone that have been dirtied in sand, a bowl of water and some cloths.

After a journey of 40 years, the people were finally ready to come to God's promised land. This was the place where they would be safe. In order to get into this land, they had one more thing to do: they needed to cross the River Jordan. It seemed impossible, but Joshua, who had taken over as leader from Moses by now, trusted God to show them how. The priests went out into the water first, carrying the great golden chest that contained the Ten Commandments (this too was called an ark), and they stood in the middle of the river. As soon as they were there, the River Jordan began to dry up so that all the people could cross safely. After many years of walking through the desert, they could walk into God's special home for them. Their feet were dusty from their desert journey but, as they crossed the wet riverbed, they were cleaned, ready for a new beginning.

Ask each child to take one of the dirty, dusty pebbles and wash it in the water. Once it is clean and dry and shiny again, oversee arranging the pebbles on the blue cloth to spell the word S-A-F-E. God's promised land was the place where his people could be safe.

## 7: Incarnation—God becomes a baby

> You will need a circle of white cloth or felt for the centre of the station (which is also the centre of the whole labyrinth), a box ready with a crib set inside and a large candle and matches.

God kept on looking after his people in the new land, but there were so many temptations to forget him and go their own way. There were great leaders and kings, such as David and Solomon, but even they didn't always choose God's way. They built special places to worship God—even a golden temple in Jerusalem—but they began to forget that God was everywhere, not just in a building. God sent special people to remind them of his love and warn them of the dangers of turning away from his love. These people were called prophets—but not everyone listened to their messages. Finally, God decided that the only way to really show his love was to come and live with his people. God decided to wrap himself up very small, and he quietly entered his own world as a tiny baby.

Build the crib scene together. Have the children tell you what happened as each of the pieces is put in place.

God had planned this all along as the way he was going to show his people what he was really like and how he could keep them safe for ever. God became a human being and his name was Jesus. In this way, he was fully human and fully God.

Light the large candle as a picture of Jesus coming as the light for the world. This candle now stands at the heart of the Bible labyrinth.

### 8: Baptism

You will need another blue circle of cloth or felt for this station of the labyrinth, to match station 6. You will also need some small tealight candles in holders (one for each child), a jug of water in a bowl and a towel.

Jesus shone bright with God's light. When he was about 30 years old he went to the River Jordan, where his cousin John was baptizing people. He asked John to baptize him. John was surprised. He knew how special Jesus was. He said it should have been Jesus baptizing him! However, Jesus insisted, and so he went down into the water and came out again. People nearby said they heard God's voice; others saw a dove coming close to Jesus. Jesus was showing everyone the way of starting a new life with God.

Invite each child (one at a time) to hold their hands over the bowl, as you pour some water over them. Once they have dried their hands, they should (with the help of an adult) light a small tealight candle, using the light from the candle at station 7, which is nearby.

The washing of baptism was a picture of how people enter into the safe place of trusting God for ever. The light reminded everyone of what it means to belong to Jesus.

### 9: The Beatitudes

You will need another grey circle of felt or cloth for this station, matching the one at station 5. You will also need some heart-shaped post-it notes and some pens and pencils.

Jesus began teaching people about God and his ways. Crowds gathered to listen. Once, he was speaking to a great crowd of men, women and children on a mountainside in Galilee. He told them about what things are like when God is king. He described the sort of lives God's people should lead. He said that people would be happy if they knew that they needed God, happy if they were sad about being far from him, and happy if they always put others first. They would be happy if they longed for what was good and right, and happy if they were kind and said 'no' to all that was bad. They would be happy if they were people who made peace. Everyone else might think they were crazy and laugh at them, but this was the only way to be happy and make God happy too.

Wonder about what the group thinks will make God really happy. Discuss this briefly with the children and then, on the heart-shaped post-it notes, invite them to write or draw the things or words that make God happy. Arrange the notes neatly on the cloth.

## 10: The Easter story

You will need another circle of green felt or cloth for this station, to match the one at station 4. You will also need five pieces of wood in exact imitation of the ones used to make the door in station 4, including the red marks, and some craft sticks (two per child) which can be tied or glued together to make a simple cross. The children will write the word JESUS along the crosspiece and RESCUER down the vertical piece, dissecting at the middle 'S' of Jesus.

Jesus said and did amazing things. Everyone knew that he was special and that he was showing them what God was like. However, very few really knew who he was. He called himself by many names. Once, he said he was the light; on other occasions he called himself the good shepherd and the way, and once he described himself as the door. *(Make a door from the pieces of wood, just like at station 4)* But Jesus knew that the only way to rescue people from the bad that keeps spoiling our lives was to go to Jerusalem and die on a cross. *(Change the door shape to become a cross, placing the red marks now where the hands and feet would be)* Now, everyone who comes to God through this cross can be safe and rescued from all that is bad. The cross gave people the power to choose to do what is right.

Invite the children to make their own cross from the craft sticks, writing on the words 'Jesus' and 'Rescuer' as described above.

## 11: The great commission

You will need a circle of sandy-coloured cloth for this station, just like the one at station 3, along with a candle in a holder and a bowl containing some sand.

After three days, Jesus was seen alive again in a new Easter way. He could now always be there for his people, to lead them into what was good and true. Although he returned to heaven, through the gift of the Holy Spirit he was still with them in a new invisible way. He wanted everyone to be filled with light as he was filled with light, and to take God's love out into the world so that more and more people would become part of God's new beginning. God's promise to Abraham was coming true. God's family was growing and growing and was becoming as many as the stars in the sky and the grains of sand in the desert.

Invite each member of the group to take a handful of sand and allow it to fall through their fingers as a picture of the huge family of God around the world today.

God wants his followers to pass on his light to others.

Pass a lighted candle around the circle carefully and slowly as a picture of what it means to pass on the light of Jesus in order to grow this family.

## 12: Holy Communion

You will need another circle of brown cloth or felt for this station, just as at station 2, as well as some cups with water and a simple biscuit for each child.

Jesus wanted everyone to remember him so that they would not forget how to come close to God wherever they were. He had given them a way to do this—not a rainbow this time, but a simple meal of bread and wine to share together. There had been bread to eat and wine to drink as part of the meal he had eaten with his friends the night before he died.

Distribute the drink and a biscuit to each member of the group, but ask them all to wait for each other so that everyone eats and drinks at the same time.

Every time Christians eat and drink in this way, they remember Jesus. They remember how he died and then came back to life to be with everyone everywhere for ever.

### 13: New creation

You need a circle of white cloth or felt for this final station of the labyrinth that contrasts with the black one at station 1. You will also need a second hexagonal set of six pieces, but this time they should all be white. You will build the hexagon with the pieces as you tell the last part of the story. Finally, you need some white paper and pencils.

The story ends with a new beginning. The first creation will be over and, because of Jesus, all that is bad and spoils God's world will be washed away. Everyone will be able to choose to be safe in Jesus. The Bible promises that God will make a new heaven and a new earth, full of light (complete the white hexagon). This is the light of God and of Jesus his Son. All that was broken will be mended and all that was painful will be healed. This is how the Bible ends, but really it is just the first page of a new book that will go on for ever. I wonder what heaven will be like?

Hand out a piece of white paper to each child and show them how to fold it to make a small concertina book. Give them some space to think as they look at this brand new book as an example of the new beginning the Bible promises.

Now, I wonder what pictures of heaven you would like to

put down here? I wonder what the next, as yet unwritten, books of the Bible will look like?

Give the children the opportunity to do some drawings, or maybe to take their paper away to work on later. Finish with the footsteps chant together (see page 199).

## Footrest

Take a break in the programme at this point for a drink and a biscuit at the team bases. This will also give time for leaders to prepare for the coming workshops.

## Footprints

The children and adults can now experience up to three different activities on a Bible theme, depending on the time available. Workshops are based around drama (Footlights), music (Footnotes) and craft (Fancy footwork).

### Footlights

1. As a warm up for this workshop, challenge the group to make a book-making machine. To do this, each person in the team chooses to become part of an imaginary machine that turns a tree into a book, adding in as many appropriate noises and actions as possible.

You will need several parts and actions for this machine, for example, cutting down a tree, sawing up the wood, pulping the wood, rolling out the pulp, cutting up the paper, printing the paper, putting together the pages, binding the book, packing up the books, delivering the books, selling the books, and finally reading a book.

Do this in an ordered way. As each new person adds to the machine, they should make their noise and/or activity on their own before all the preceding noises and actions strike up simultaneously.

**2.** Below are some outlines for possible mime presentations for various Bible stories. Choose some that are suitable for the age range of the group. Perhaps the leader could arrange, over the course of about three workshops, to build up a set that could be presented to everyone later as 'the Bible in mime'.

You will need some chairs (one for every member of the group in the last scene).

## The Old Testament

The first mime represents the story of creation and then the story of the first sin. Two people lie on the ground while a third person (the creator) first hovers over them and then steps back. The two people stand up and join hands with the creator, one on either side so that the creator stands in the middle. After a pause, one of the two created beings looks away from the creator, lets go and moves away. Soon after, the second created being also lets go and moves away. The three should now stand with the creator on one side and the two created beings on the other. The creator then takes a chair and stands on it, high and separate from the other two. The creator remains on this chair for the rest of the Old Testament mimes.

The second mime represents God choosing Abraham and Sarah. The creator (standing on the chair) mimes calling out to people. Two people walk by and respond by listening (hand to ears) and then by walking around the chair as they 'travel' together, sometimes pausing to kneel.

The third mime represents God choosing Moses. The creator on the chair beckons with his or her hands. One actor comes close, but is afraid. The actor takes off his or her shoes, listens and then walks away, but returns to walk around the chair.

The fourth mime represents the escape from Egypt. The creator on the chair points firmly into the distance, away from where the other children are standing. The children are all close together, fiercely guarded by one other person. The person who was beckoned to in the last scene (Moses) approaches, and points in the same direction as the creator. The creator then counts slowly to ten on his or her hands. When ten is reached, the person guarding the other children steps aside so that they can follow Moses in the direction in which the creator is pointing.

The fifth mine represents Moses receiving the Ten Commandments and the years that the people of Israel spent wandering in the desert. The creator on the chair is writing, in big letters. The other children walk away from the chair and back again four times, pausing each time they are close to the chair to listen to the person who is writing.

The sixth mime represents God choosing David to be king of Israel. The creator on the chair enacts pouring out oil from a flask (anointing) and then holds his or her hands out in blessing. The children look at each other uncertainly, and then one of them stands up above the others while the others crouch down.

The seventh mime represents God's people worshipping at the temple built by Solomon. The creator on the chair listens intently with his or her hand to an ear. The other children circle the chair, lift their hands in worship and then bow to the ground.

The eighth mime represents God's prophets calling the people back to God. The creator on the chair pushes forward with open hands, as if sending people. All the others are crouching. From time to time, some stand and point toward the chair; then others stand and point in a different direction.

### The New Testament

The first mime represents the story of Christmas. The person who was standing on the chair now steps down and very deliberately crouches down among the others, who are sitting on the floor. Most look away; just three turn and look.

The second mime represents Jesus choosing his disciples. The person who stepped down from the chair (the Christ figure) now stands up and, one by one, the others stand up and follow him. Together they walk in a circle around the chair, following the Christ figure.

The third mime represents Jesus' teaching. The Christ figure now stands in the middle while the others sit, looking up and listening.

The fourth mime represents Jesus' last meal with his friends. The Christ figure stands centrally with head bowed, while the others, sitting around, reach out towards him or her. The Christ figure mimes breaking bread and pouring wine to share.

The fifth mime represents the story of Good Friday. The Christ figure stands with arms held out as if on a cross. The others move far away, except for one who stays and stands close.

The sixth mime represents the resurrection. All are sitting with heads bowed. Suddenly the person among them who is the Christ figure stands up, and the others react with amazement.

The seventh mime represents the great commission and the ascension. The Christ figure now goes back to the chair to stand on it, and points slowly in every compass direction. The others gather round in a circle and follow the pointing with their eyes. Those around the chair then begin to spread out wider and wider, moving into every corner of the room and pointing to the Christ figure from where they are.

The eighth mime represents the new heavens and the new earth. Each of the people around the room now picks up a chair and moves to draw close to the Christ figure on the central chair. Now they, too, stand on chairs around Jesus. All lift their hands in praise. Then they all reach out and join hands, including Jesus, in God's new beginning.

This mime of the story of the Bible has been kept as simple as possible. It may be that some sort of one-line narration is thought appropriate to go alongside each scene, but it can be very powerful if people are left to work out the story for themselves. Not all details of facial expressions and movements have been recorded here, but any group that practises this mime will begin to add some of their own and thereby make the mime more effective.

If your group are readers, print off the different instructions for the different mimes and give groups the opportunity to rehearse particular sections.

## Footnotes

Have a selection of instruments available with which to experiment. Decide which kind of sounds best express the various types of books found in the Bible. For example, there might be warning drums for the prophets, stringed instruments for the love poetry, cymbals for the history books, brass instruments for the books of the law, keyboard sounds for the letters and recorders for the Gospels. Can the group create a sound version of the Bible in this way?

There are a number of Bible-linked songs that you could also teach and sing together, such as:

I am so glad that my Father in heaven (with the line 'wonderful things in the Bible I see') (*Junior Praise* 88)
The best book to read is the Bible (*Junior Praise* 234)
Every day with Jesus (Ishmael, Glorie music), beginning 'I realize the Bible is the book I need to read'
God's way (Nick Harding), beginning 'Take the Bible, live it out'
When we walk with the Lord (perhaps just verse 1 and chorus) (*Mission Praise* 760)
I will sing the wondrous story (*Junior Praise* 127)
Make the book live to me, O Lord (*Junior Praise* 163)
The wise man built his house on the rock (*Junior Praise* 252)
Don't build your house on the sandy land (*Junior Praise* 39)

## Fancy footwork

The following idea is for making a small pocket-sized Bible-like book, which is also a secret treasure box.

Remove the outer sleeve from the matchbox and cut it open along one of the edges. Turn it over so that the plain side is uppermost and wrap it around the inner drawer of the matchbox. Stick the outer sleeve on to the drawer on the back and one side, leaving the front section free to open up. (You will need to work on the creases appropriately to enable the sleeve to hinge easily.) The outer sleeve should overlap by a small amount the inner drawer of the box, in the way that a hardback cover is bigger than the inside pages of a book.

Next, take some gold paper along which you have drawn a number of lines very close together in pencil. Cut the paper into pieces that will stick neatly on to the exposed side of the inner drawer, to give the effect of gold pages.

The outer sleeve can then be coloured and decorated. In bright letters, put a title on the front of the book (and possibly also along the spine), such as 'My Pocket Bible', 'God's Special Book' or 'The Big Story'.

Inside this 'book', there is room for some small objects, which could symbolize some particular Bible stories from the day. Perhaps you could include a small wooden cross or a thin white birthday candle for Jesus, a stone to represent the Ten Commandments and a star for the promise given to Abraham. The children might like to put something of their own here as a reminder of the part of the event that they liked the best.

# Foothold

Use the footsteps chant (see page 199) to bring everyone back to the team bases for a final time of prayer and reflection. The teams should sit in a circle with their leaders, who have placed a Bible at the centre. Open the Bible up at Psalm 119, which is all about God's words.

The Bible writers describe God's words in several ways. As the central leader speaks each line of the following section, each team leader should place the appropriate objects in a circle around the open Bible.

**Leader:** The Bible is like a light. It shines to show us the best path to take in life.

*Place a candle or a lantern around the Bible.*

**Leader:** The Bible is like a treasure chest. It is full of riches from God for us.

*Place a small golden box around the Bible.*

**Leader:** The Bible is like food. We need to read it regularly to stay spiritually alive.

*Place a bread roll around the Bible.*

**Leader:** The Bible is like honey. It is sweet and good for us, bringing health.

*Place a small jar of honey around the Bible.*

**Leader:** The Bible is like a sword. It can help us to fight all that is bad.

*Place a small model sword around the Bible.*

Reproduced with permission from *Footsteps to the Feast* published by BRF 2007 (978 1 84101 464 7).

**Leader:** The Bible is like a conversation with God. It can help us to hear what he is saying.

*Place a mobile phone around the Bible.*

**Leader:** God's special book for us shows us how to live life as God planned. The big story of the Bible helps us find our way through the story of our lives. *(Pause)*

I wonder which description of the Bible you like the best?

*Allow some time for their response or else some quiet wondering. Pause.*

**Leader:** Help us, Father, to get to know your Bible better. As we read it, help us to hear you speaking to us. Thank you for the Bible. Amen

## Footsteps to the feast

As a finale, gather all the children in a great circle. The big story of the Bible has been passed on from generation to generation. Now it is our turn to pass it on.

Hand out some Bibles to one or two children at various points in the circle. The idea now is to pass the Bible on (clockwise) to the next person in as many different ways as possible. Demonstrate some possible ways, such as passing it on mysteriously, presenting it as a prize, opening it up and pointing to a verse, pretending to sing from it, acting out part of a story, passing it over the shoulder or under the arm and so on. Give everyone a chance to think of a fun method and then, on the count of three, start the Bibles being passed around the circle as fast as possible until they have all returned back to where they started.

Finish with the footsteps chant for the day (see page 199).

## Stepping out

End the event with a Bible feast together, inviting parents and carers to join you for food and drink. Perhaps you might have a cake in the shape of a big book, or small biscuits or cakes decorated with iced verses or Bible-related words.

# Star lampshade

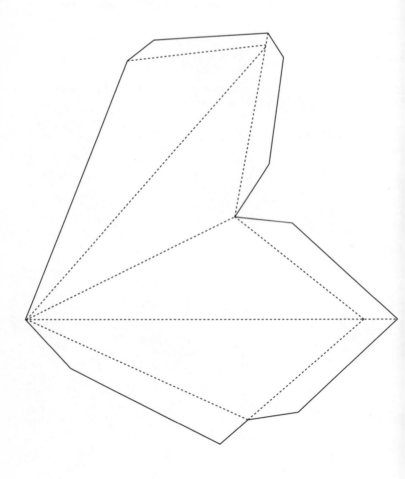

# Dove mobile

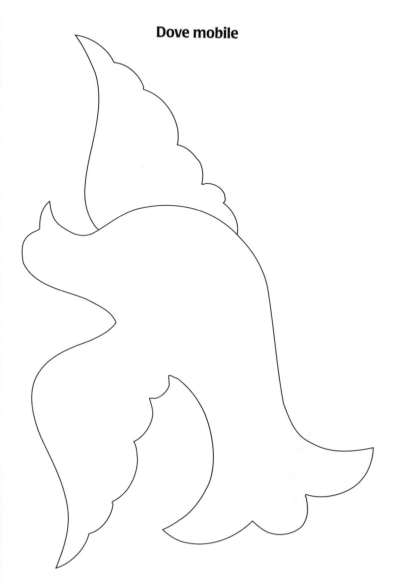

# Flame template

# Bible labyrinth

# Bible index

Genesis 1:16 .............................35
Genesis 6:1—9:17.....................202
Genesis 8:21–22 ......................142
Genesis 9:8–13 ........................142
Genesis 9:12–17 ......................156
Genesis 12:1–9 ..........................36
Genesis 12:3b ............................18
Genesis 15:5 ..............................35
Genesis 18:1–15 ......................119
Genesis 18:1–16 ......................180
Genesis 18:14 ..........................180
Genesis 22:13–14 ......................21
Genesis 22:17 ............................21
Genesis 28:12 ..........................190
Genesis 32:22–32 ....................190
Genesis 37:1–4 ........................202
Genesis 49:9–10 ........................21
Exodus 3:1–10 .........................161
Exodus 3:11–13 .......................167
Exodus 4:1, 10 ........................167
Exodus 13:21–22 .....................181
Exodus 14:19–20 .....................181
Exodus 14:21–22 .....................202
Exodus 19:16–25 .....................202
Exodus 23:20 ...........................181
Numbers 22:21–35 ...................181
Numbers 22:27–28 ...................181
Deuteronomy 18:15a....................18
Deuteronomy 18:18.......................21
Deuteronomy 26:1–11.................142
Joshua 6:6–20 ..........................202
Judges 16:20 ...........................202
Ruth 1:1–2 ..............................150
Ruth 1:3–5 ..............................150
Ruth 1:6–18 ............................151
Ruth 2:1–16 ............................151
Ruth 3:1–18 ............................152
Ruth 4:1–12 ............................152
Ruth 4:13–17 ..........................152
1 Samuel 17:41–50 ...................202

1 Kings 9:5 ...............................18
2 Kings 6:11–23 .......................180
2 Kings 6:16 ............................180
2 Chronicles 32:1–23 ................181
2 Chronicles 32:21 ...................181
Job 38:7 ....................................45
Psalm 1:3................................142
Psalm 67 .................................142
Psalm 89:19...............................18
Psalm 89:27–29...........................21
Psalm 103:20............................188
Psalm 148:2.............................188
Psalm 119:18, 105.....................195
Isaiah 5:1–5 ............................142
Isaiah 6:1–8.....................181, 188
Isaiah 6:1–11.............................24
Isaiah 6:3................................181
Isaiah 7:3..................................24
Isaiah 7:13–17............................24
Isaiah 8:1–4..............................24
Isaiah 9:6............................18, 21
Isaiah 9:6–7...............................24
Isaiah 11:6.................................21
Isaiah 40:3.................................21
Isaiah 40:11...............................21
Isaiah 40:26...............................45
Isaiah 43:1...............................137
Isaiah 43:4...............................137
Isaiah 48:18.............................142
Isaiah 62:2.................................21
Isaiah 58:11.............................142
Jeremiah 23:5 ............................18
Jeremiah 23:5–6 .........................21
Jeremiah 29:11 .........................137
Daniel 3:1–30 ..........................119
Daniel 6:1–23 ..........................202
Daniel 12:3 ...............................35
Jonah 1:13–17...........................202
Micah 5:2 .................................18
Micah 5:2–3 ..............................21

Matthew 2:1–12 ......................38, 119
Matthew 3 .......................................111
Matthew 4:1–11 ..............................65
Matthew 5:16 ..................................50
Matthew 17:1–8 ............................119
Matthew 18:10 ..............................179
Matthew 21—28 ............................80
Matthew 28:10 ..............................137
Matthew 28:20 ..............................137
Mark 1:4–11 ..................................111
Mark 6:45–52 ................................202
Mark 11–16....................................80
Mark 14:3–9 ..................................87
Luke 1:5—2:19 ..............................17
Luke 1:54–55 .................................19
Luke 1:69 .......................................19
Luke 2:1–7 ....................................202
Luke 2:22–38 .................................51
Luke 3:1–22 ..................................111
Luke 15:10 ....................................192
Luke 19:1–10 ................................202
Luke 19:28—24:53 .........................80
John 1:5 .........................................160
John 1:19–34 ................................111
John 1:42 .......................................137

John 12:1–3 ....................................87
John 12—20 ....................................80
John 13:1–14 ..................................87
John 14:18 .....................................137
John 15:1–10 .................................142
John 15:15 .....................................137
Acts 2:1–42 .....................................96
Acts 4:32–37 .................................127
Acts 9:26–30 .................................127
Acts 11:19–30 ...............................127
Acts 13 ..........................................127
Acts 27:23 .....................................179
Acts 27:39–44 ...............................202
Romans 15:4 .................................194
Galatians 4:4 ...........................20, 194
Galatians 5:22–23 .........................108
Ephesians 3:14–16, 20 ..................100
2 Timothy 3:16 .............................194
Hebrews 1:7 ..................................179
Hebrews 1:1–7 ..............................180
Hebrews 13:2 ................................181
1 Peter 1:12...................................179
1 John 1:5, 7 ..................................161
Revelation 1:16 ..............................35
Revelation 22:16 ............................35

# Bibliography

## Barnabas books for Advent

*Easy Ways to Christmas Plays*, Vicki Howie (includes three nativity plays)

*Practical Ways to Christmas Plays*, Stephanie Jeffs (includes five nativity plays)

*Nursery Rhyme Nativities*, Brian Ogden (includes three nativity plays especially for younger children)

*Topsy Turvy Christmas*, Lucy Moore (a musical nativity with some great new songs available on CD or as MP3 downloads)

*Story Plays for Christmas*, Vicki Howie (includes three more nativity plays for Key Stage 2 children)

*Celebrations Make & Do*, Gillian Chapman (for making a special Advent garland)

*Christmas Make & Do*, Gillian Chapman (ten craft ideas including an Advent calendar and a recipe for Christmas cookies)

*Bible Make & Do 3*, Gillian Chapman (includes a nativity crib for Advent)

*Bible Make & Do 4*, Gillian Chapman (includes an idea for a shepherds' surprise Christmas card)

*Step-by-Step Christmas Crib* (full instructions for a model nativity scene)

*Christmas Fun*, Leena Lane (seasonal puzzles, mazes and pictures to colour in)

*Walking with Jesus through Advent and Christmas*, Murray McBride (all-age reflections and colouring activities)

## Christmas gift books

*Look and See: The Story of Jesus*, Leena Lane

*Bible Explorer: Jesus is Born*, Stephanie Jeffs and Jenny Tulip

*Bible Explorer: The Life of Jesus*, Stephanie Jeffs and Jenny Tulip

## Books for Lent

*Through the Year with Timothy Bear*, Brian Sears (five-minute stories for the seasons of the year with follow-up activities)

*High-Energy Holiday Club Songs* CD, John Hardwick (for 'God's people aren't superbrave superheroes' and 'God so loved the world')

## Books for Trinity

*Celebrations Make & Do*, Gillian Chapman (for a Trinity mosaic)

*Through the Year with Timothy Bear*, Brian Sears (five-minute stories for the seasons of the year with follow-up activities)

## Books for Harvest

*Celebrations Make & Do*, Gillian Chapman (for a harvest banner)

## Books for All Saints

*Celebrations Make & Do* (includes instructions for a golden incense bowl craft idea)

*Bible Make & Do 2* (includes instructions for a clay lamp craft idea)

*Bible Make & Do 3* (includes instructions for a golden lamp stand craft idea)

## Books for St Michael and All Angels

Barnabas books containing angel songs, in particular linked to the Christmas story include *Nursery Rhyme Nativities* and *Topsy Turvy Christmas*.

For further inspiration about angels, see the following books by Bob Hartman. He imagines each angel as having a particular character suited to the work he is called to do:

*Angels, Angels Everywhere*
*The Easter Angels*
*The Night the Stars Danced for Joy*

A further series of books from America by Gene Edwards, called *The Chronicles of the Door* trace the story of the Bible from the angels' perspective.

## Music resources

Junior Praise
Mission Praise
Kidsource
Big Blue Planet
Psalm Praise

# ★ Also from BRF ★

# A-cross the World

An exploration of 40 representations of the cross
from the worldwide Christian Church

## Martyn Payne and Betty Pedley

Around the world today the cross is, arguably, the one universally recognized symbol of the Christian faith, but this unifying sign for diverse Christian communities has been much adapted, decorated and interpreted to convey particular stories that are dear to the community from which they come.

This book tells the stories behind 40 crosses from a wide diversity of cultures and Christian faith traditions and sets out to promote discussion and debate on why this single, historical event continues to exercise such an influence worldwide.

Section One contains stories, information, Bible links, wondering questions and suggested activities on the 40 crosses, as well as photocopiable illustrations of each cross. The material for this section was originally produced by the Church Mission Society.

Section Two contains a wealth of extension material ideal for use in the classroom at Key Stage 1 and 2, in collective worship and in church-based activities, including icebreakers, games, prayers and poems, crafts and session outlines for special activity days, assemblies, holiday clubs and all-age worship.

*ISBN 978 1 84101 264 3   £15.99*
*Available from your local Christian bookshop or, in case of difficulty, direct from BRF using the order form on page 239.*

### ★ Also from BRF ★

# Not Sunday, Not School!

Through-the-year children's programmes
for small churches

## Eleanor Zuercher

Many churches, particularly those with small congregations and even smaller numbers of children attending on a Sunday morning, struggle with the traditional model of Sunday school and long to find a way to work with more children more effectively. This book sets out to show that, with a bit of lateral and creative thinking, perceived weaknesses can become strengths, with the end result that children's work, even in a small church, can become vibrant and successful.

*Not Sunday, Not School!* is packed with ideas and activities for an alternative model to the traditional Sunday school. The material comprises tried and tested two-hour thematic programmes that will take you right the way through the Christian year, plus an alternative programme for Hallowe'en and a series for a five-day holiday club programme, or stand-alone workshops for the summer months.

Each session includes suggestions for Bible stories based on the theme, suggestions for creating a display for the church, craft activities, games and suggestions for prayer.

*ISBN 978 1 84101 490 6   £9.99*
*Available from your local Christian bookshop or, in case of difficulty, direct from BRF using the order form on page 239.*

★ **Also from BRF** ★

# Core Skills
# for Children's Work

Developing and extending key skills for children's ministry

## The Consultative Group on Ministry among Children

Building on the huge success of the original *Kaleidoscope* course published by NCEC in 1993, this exciting new interdenominational modular scheme offers foundational training for all those involved with church-based children's ministry and addresses the six areas of expertise set out by the DfES in the Common Core of Skills and Knowledge for the Children's Workforce.

The material draws on the expertise of a wide ecumenical team under the guidance of the Consultative Group on Ministry among Children (CGMC) and comprises stand-alone modules in six key areas: child development, leadership skills, programme planning, children and community, pastoral awareness, and spirituality and the Bible.

All six modules have been thoroughly field-tested as two-hour training programmes in ecumenical pilot groups. Each module is creative, thought-provoking, interactive and designed to inspire and refresh children's workers at all levels of expertise and experience.

*ISBN 978 1 84101 507 1   £12.99*
*Available from your local Christian bookshop or, in case of difficulty, direct from BRF using the order form on page 239.*

## ORDER FORM

| REF | TITLE | PRICE | QTY | TOTAL |
|---|---|---|---|---|
| 264 3 | A-cross the World | £15.99 | | |
| 490 6 | Not Sunday, Not School! | £9.99 | | |
| 507 1 | Core Skills for Children's Workers | £12.99 | | |

| POSTAGE AND PACKING CHARGES | | | | | | |
|---|---|---|---|---|---|---|
| Order value | UK | Europe | Surface | Air Mail | Postage and packing: | |
| £7.00 & under | £1.25 | £3.00 | £3.50 | £5.50 | Donation: | |
| £7.01–£30.00 | £2.25 | £5.50 | £6.50 | £10.00 | Total enclosed: | |
| Over £30.00 | free | prices on request | | | | |

Name _____ Account Number _____

Address _____

_____ Postcode _____

Telephone Number _____ Email _____

Payment by: ❑ Cheque ❑ Mastercard ❑ Visa ❑ Postal Order ❑ Maestro

Card no. ❑❑❑❑ ❑❑❑❑ ❑❑❑❑ ❑❑❑❑

Expires ❑❑ ❑❑ Security code ❑❑❑ Issue no. ❑❑❑

Signature _____ Date _____

*All orders must be accompanied by the appropriate payment.*

**Please send your completed order form to:**
BRF, 15 The Chambers, Vineyard, Abingdon OX14 3FE
Tel. 01865 319700 / Fax. 01865 319701 Email: enquiries@brf.org.uk

❑ Please send me further information about BRF publications.

Available from your local Christian bookshop.          BRF is a Registered Charity

## Resourcing people to work with 3–11s
in churches and schools

- Articles, features, ideas
- Training and events
- Books and resources
- www.barnabasinchurches.org.uk

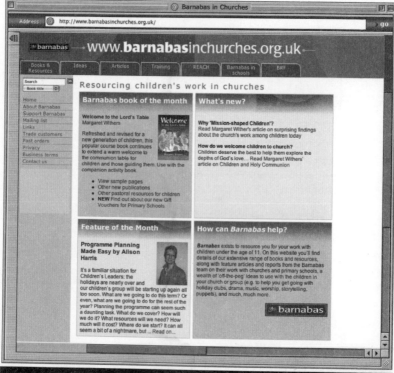